MURDER OF A GENTLE LAND

MURDER OF A
GENTLE LAND

The Untold Story of Communist
Genocide in Cambodia

John Barron and Anthony Paul

Research Associates: Katherine Clark and Ursula Naccache

READER'S DIGEST PRESS
Distributed by
Thomas Y. Crowell Company   New York   1977

LIBRARY OF CONGRESS CATALOGING IN PUBLICATION DATA

Barron, John, 1930–
    Murder of a gentle land.

    Bibliography: p.
    Includes index.
    1. Political atrocities—Cambodia. 2. Cambodia
—Politics and government. I. Paul, Anthony, joint
author. II. Title.
DS554.8.B37   320.9'596'04   77-1060
ISBN 0-88349-129-X

10   9   8   7   6   5   4   3   2

CONTENTS

PREFACE

Many of the events recounted in this book reflect a horror difficult to comprehend in terms of the personal experiences most of us have had, and because the horror is so alien, it tends to be incredible. Therefore, we have felt obligated to identify in Chapter Notes the sources of data on which each chapter is based. And to enable readers further to assess the accuracy and validity of our reporting, we also consider ourselves obligated to explain in some detail how the book was conceived, researched and written.

The decision to publish a book about Cambodia resulted from two separate proposals that by coincidence reached the editors of the *Reader's Digest* on the same day, September 8, 1975.

The preceding July managing editor Kenneth Gilmore sent me a routine handwritten note: "I keep seeing fragmentary reports that suggest something terrible may be taking place in Cambodia. Please find out what you can and let me have your recommendations." Accordingly, I sought and received informal briefings from specialists at the State and Defense Departments, the National Security Council and three foreign embassies in Washington. These diverse sources all stated that the communist conquerors of Cambodia had banished life from the cities, marched the entire urban population into the countryside and put virtually everybody to work tilling the soil under deathly conditions. There were substantial indications that innumerable men, women and children had perished as a consequence of exposure, disease, hunger, executions and massacres. It seemed as if the new regime was determined, regardless of human or material cost, to obliterate every vestige of past Cambodian civilization so as to create out of a void a society totally of its own making. Summarizing these briefings, I concluded that if through independent research we could verify and document what appeared to be happening in Cambodia, the resultant story might be of sufficient magnitude and import to justify a book.

Meanwhile, Roving Editor Anthony Paul, based in Hong Kong, had been making an assessment of the Cambodian situation on his own initiative. Tony had visited Cambodia as a war correspondent. He witnessed the final siege of Phnom Penh and was one of the foreigners evacuated by helicopter on April 12, 1975, five days before the capital fell. An assignment subsequently took him to refugee camps on Guam, and among thousands of Vietnamese there he encountered a few Cambodians who had escaped after the communist conquest. The atrocities and other inhumanities they claimed to have seen were so barbaric that Tony could not quite believe their accounts. Cambodia now had sealed itself off into a hostile hermit kingdom inaccessible to foreigners. So Tony talked to the best outside sources he could locate in the Far East, including his contacts in Asian governments from Japan to Thailand. By August he was convinced that the developments in Cambodia constituted an untold story of enduring, worldwide significance.

Neither Tony nor I was aware of the surveys being made by the other. We consulted disparate sources of different nationalities on opposite sides of the world. Yet our findings and recommendations were virtually identical.

Having arrived simultaneously from Washington and Hong Kong, our respective presentations were considered immediately by Ken Gilmore and Roy Herbert, the managing editor with whom Tony worked. Two days later Ken telephoned to inform me of their reactions. Both agreed the story as described to them represented such an important episode in contemporary history that every effort should be made to document and narrate it in the form of a book as quickly as possible. Both felt that were Tony and I to collaborate, it could be completed much more quickly than if either of us undertook the project alone.

To formulate research procedures in the early days of the project, Tony and I conferred often and at length by both telephone and correspondence. We first identified the sources that might yield data, and they fell into five general categories.

Virtually the only available eyewitnesses to life inside Cambodia were the refugees who continued to flee through the jungles into Thailand. Although some were being resettled in France and the United States, most were still lodged in camps along the Thai-Cambodian border. We knew that we could rely significantly on testimony from refugees only if we interviewed a large number from varied social strata and geographic locales over a protracted period of time. And we determined that we would have to tape-record and transcribe all substantive interviews in order to prove that testimony attributed to refugees had actually been given.

The daily broadcasts of Radio Phnom Penh and pronouncements of the new Cambodian leaders represented a second potential source of information. While recognizing the difficulty of distinguishing fact from propaganda, we reasoned that the communist regime might reveal much about itself if we listened closely and carefully enough.

Scholars, in and out of government, who had specialized in Cambodian affairs offered a third source of help. We thought that by virtue of their special interest and involvement in the country, they could discern in information acquired through their own channels or information we shared meaning that otherwise might escape us.

Endeavoring to read all that had been published about Cambodia, we failed to find any news organization or publication that was making a continuing, concerted effort to report what was transpiring in the country. But individual journalists now and then were filing enlightening dispatches, usually based on interviews with a few newly arrived refugees in Thailand. We felt that the reports of other journalists could provide a yardstick of some use in evaluating our own findings. So we resolved to read and analyze every scrap of information that the international offices of the *Digest* could glean from the world press.

Intelligence collected by foreign governments about Cambodia constituted a fifth prospective source of information. We anticipated that any secret intelligence we might obtain almost certainly would be provided only on a confidential basis and could not be used for purposes of documentation. Nevertheless, we felt it would be valuable to check our own data against those amassed by assorted governments.

Realizing that the two of us could not adequately exploit all these resources, we requested that Katharine Clark, a researcher in the *Digest's* Washington office, and Ursula Naccache, an associate editor in the European editorial office in Paris, be made partners in the project.

For more than twenty years Katharine had distinguished herself as a foreign correspondent in Europe and Asia before joining the *Digest* in 1967. Working with me on a previous book and numerous articles, she had further demonstrated herself to be a gifted journalist with rare ability to organize research data and locate people able to answer perplexing questions. Katharine was to maintain our central repository of data, analyze Radio Phnom Penh broadcasts and other communist statements, interview refugees coming to the United States, as well as American scholars.

Ursula had participated in some of the most important research projects sponsored by the *Digest* in the past fifteen years and contributed much to the late Cornelius Ryan's highly acclaimed *The Longest Day*. Her reports consistently were masterpieces of scholarship and exposition. Ursula was exhaustively to interview Cambodians entering France and to enlist the cooperation of French scholars and authorities, particularly those whose views might differ from those of their counterparts in America and the Far East. And we wanted her, together with Katharine, to subject the final manuscript to rigorous checking and help oversee its documentation.

In October Tony and I, accompanied by two interpreters, arrived at the refugee camp in Aranyaprathet near the Cambodian border after a five-hour drive east from Bangkok. The camp consisted of warehouselike structures with open sides and tin or thatched roofs. Each family was allotted a small space which was walled off by blankets strung from clothesline. The camp was a babble of noise. Children were crying, mothers trying to comfort distraught infants were crooning lullabies, roosters were crowing and from a nearby temple came the sound of a gong. A sickly stench born of charcoal fires, open sewers, unwashed bodies and rancid cooking oil pervaded the air. Sitting on the floor in one of these spaces, we conducted one of the first interviews with a truck driver, Ith Thaim, who told of the scene described on page 83. He had watched as ten families comprising about sixty people were stabbed and bludgeoned to death in a banana grove, family by family, the men first, the women next and the children and babies last.

After recording other awful testimony throughout the day, Tony and I settled for the night in primitive bungalows near the frontier. There had been firefights between Thai and Cambodian patrols, between police and smugglers, and now and then we heard the flat, staccato pops of automatic rifle fire. We wanted nothing to eat, and we were so overcome with emotion that we could not sleep, so we listened to tapes of our interviews.

We wondered how we and our own wives and children would have reacted had all of us been in the place of the families in the banana grove. We spoke of the Cambodians we had just seen, people whose traumatized faces and emaciated bodies bore the scars of the hell from which they had emerged. Ultimately that evening we knew and acknowledged that our greatest challenge was control of our own emotions. So we pledged that we would conduct all interviews as clinically, skeptically, professionally and in as detached a manner as possible. We would identify personally with no refugee, no matter how pitiable or appealing; we would offer no one any inducement to talk to us. There would be not a single tear, at least not until the last word was written.

With the help of Saner Khettasiri of the Thai Ministry of the Interior, we gained access in October and November to four refugee camps from which journalists had been banned. In each, our methods were the same. We approached the camp leader elected by the Cambodians and from his knowledge of his people compiled a list of refugees who seemed to be promising subjects. Then we talked informally to each, assessing credibility, intelligence, background and experiences, before deciding whether to interview the refugee at length.

By the time we returned to Bangkok in November we had spoken to more than 100 Cambodians and recorded fifty-nine interviews. These were only a beginning, but they supplied enough knowledge to enable us tentatively to outline the book. We agreed that

Tony would return to the Thai camps every couple of months while from Washington I would coordinate research in France and the United States. And on the basis of our outline we divided responsibility for various chapters.

Between October 1975 and October 1976 the four of us talked with more than 300 Cambodian refugees in Thailand, Malaysia, France and the United States and transcribed more than half the interviews. Several times Ursula in France reinterviewed Cambodians whom Tony or I had interrogated in Thailand in an attempt to verify or amplify their accounts. Concerning basic conditions in Cambodia, we found a remarkable consistency in the testimony of the refugees, no matter when, where or by whom they were interviewed.

Someone, perhaps Joseph Stalin, is reputed to have said, "One death is a tragedy; a million deaths are a statistic." In writing the book, we have tried to tell of a million deaths and more in a way that would not make them just a statistic. We believed we would be more likely to succeed if we understated the reality our research proved to us existed. That we have endeavored to do. Wherever the facts allowed, we also attempted to illuminate the experiences of millions by re-creating the experiences of individuals typical of these millions.

It was not our purpose to detail, much less debate, the history of the Indochina war that preceded the communist conquest in Cambodia. The book, rather, is concerned with what has happened in Cambodia since April 17, 1975, and we have referred to prior events only to the extent we thought such references were necessary to an understanding of what has transpired since then.

The documentation appears in Chapter Notes at the end of the book. There we identify our sources, most of whom are the refugees whose words are recorded on tapes we retain. In the Khmer language the surname precedes the given name; however, Cambodians customarily address each other by their first names. In consonance with Western usage, we have referred to individuals, except children, by their surnames. A few refugees, fearing reprisals against their families still in Cambodia, consented to be interviewed only on the condition that we disguise their names.

We believe that the documentation conclusively shows that cataclysmic events have occurred in Cambodia and that their occurrence is not subject to rational dispute. We hope that upon learning of these events, people in all parts of the world will act to halt the ongoing annihilation of the Cambodian people and to spare the world a repetition of their tragedy.

JOHN BARRON
Annandale, Virginia
December 1, 1976

I

PEACE
DAWNS

Peace came to the once-lovely land of Cambodia on the morning of April 17, 1975. After five years of civil war the government under General Lon Nol had collapsed, the army had disintegrated, the last American diplomats had fled. As dawn streaked the sky with brilliant hues of pink, blue, orange, and gold, the besieged capital of Phnom Penh lay prostrate and defenseless before encircling communist forces. Radio Phnom Penh was silent again, and in the absence of communiqués from either the government or the insurgents the 3,000,000 people crowded into the capital could not be sure of what was happening.* But many sensed the war was over at about 6 A.M., when

---

*Both communist sources, such as Cambodian Foreign Minister Ieng Sary, and responsible noncommunist sources, such as the *Far Eastern Economic Review*, have stated that the population of Phnom Penh at the end of the war was 3,000,000. Western intelli-

the communists ceased bombarding the city with Chinese rockets.

These 107 millimeter rockets had tortured the capital almost continuously ever since the siege began in January. The wobbly 107 announces its arrival with an eerie, unnerving whoosh. Upon impact, 20 kilograms of steel and explosives burst into thousands of shreds of jagged white-hot shrapnel that kill or maim anybody within 23 meters. The communists preferred to fire the 107s at markets, street intersections, temples, schools or wherever people were likely to congregate. It did not matter that most of the victims inevitably were civilians, particularly the poor, who frequented the streets. For the rockets were aimed not so much at individuals or physical targets as at the minds of the populace. Their purpose, which they achieved to a considerable degree, was to provoke popular revulsion against the war and the government whose continued resistance perpetuated the war.

In the random death and mutilation inflicted by the bombardment, the people had seen the ugly, senseless cruelty of war. Now, in the cessation of the bombardment, they beheld an instant and merciful blessing of peace, and they were grateful. Men, women and children by the tens of thousands broke

---

gence sources consulted by the authors also believe that the capital contained at least this many people.

However, the figure 3,000,000 represents only an enlightened estimate. The population of Phnom Penh swelled steadily as people fled the countryside, and the influx was especially heavy in the final weeks of fighting. During those last weeks neither the Lon Nol government nor anyone else was in a position to count the population.

the government curfew and ventured into the suddenly safe streets or climbed on roofs to await and welcome the communists. Rumors told them they should signify their acceptance of peace by displaying white flags, and quickly the city blossomed with emblems of surrender. Families draped white sheets from windows and strung white shawls or white shirts from trees before their homes. Girls put white ribbons in their hair; men and boys tied strips of white cloth to the handlebars of bicycles and the antennas of automobiles; people of all ages wrapped white handkerchiefs around their arms. Merchants hung white towels from their stores, and the Cambodian Electricity Company hoisted white pillowcases above its offices.

The first communist squads, each composed of ten to twelve soldiers, were spotted infiltrating the capital at about 7 A.M. The soldiers, mute and phlegmatic, walked in single file from the outskirts and proceeded warily down main thoroughfares, seemingly uncertain of exactly where they were headed. In general, they were small men and women from peasant stock dressed in black pajamalike uniforms, peaked Mao caps and Ho Chi Minh sandals carved from rubber tires. Thoroughly encrusted with the grime and smell of the jungles they long had inhabited, most looked tired, gaunt and tough. Some were only thirteen or fourteen years old and scarcely taller than the Chinese AK-47 or American M-16 rifles they carried. Yet even these children were often combat veterans, having been impressed into the revolutionary army at age ten or eleven when the communists had overrun their villages.

Larger detachments of troops soon entered the city

from the northwest and southwest. While a few rode in jeeps or trucks, many arranged their own transportation by commandeering vehicles of all varieties wherever they found them. Before long a goodly portion of the army of occupation was spreading through Phnom Penh in pedicabs, bicycles, motorbikes, motorcycles, taxicabs, government jeeps, personnel carriers and General Motors trucks and in confiscated black Mercedes, yellow Citroëns and aging Peugeots.

At the sight of the communists, clusters of people along the streets clapped and cheered, and even some Buddhist monks standing in their long saffron robes joined in the applause. Small children darted among the soldiers, yelling, "The war is over! The war is over!" Adults shouted, "Bravo! . . . "Congratulations, comrade!" . . . "Victory!" . . . "Peace!   Peace!" . . . "Let's shake hands!" . . . "Long live peace! Long live peace!" Women threw garlands of yellow blossoms, couples danced in the streets and sang Khmer folk songs, and teenagers beat drums in a steady tattoo of exultation.

In all their obeisances and rejoicing, the people were not necessarily celebrating the victory of communism as such. Indeed, there is no evidence that the communists ever enjoyed the voluntary support of more than a small minority of Cambodians, in either the countryside or the cities. The collectivizations and harsh regimen of life they imposed in conquered territories alienated the peasantry affected. As the communists expanded their control of the countryside, more and more families fled to the cities until a mass migration resulted. At the beginning of the war, in 1970, only about 13 percent of the nation's 7,000,000 citizens lived in urban areas. By spring

1975 the cities had absorbed more than half the national population. Some refugees brought with them reports that the communists had beaten village headmen to death with hammers, beheaded Buddhist monks, knifed children to death, slaughtered whole families and razed entire villages. Even the majority who had never heard such atrocity stories or who disbelieved them still viewed communism with indifference, skepticism or hostility.

However, if the communists did not command widespread allegiance, neither did the Lon Nol government. It was notoriously incompetent and conspicuously corrupt. By means both crude and ingenious, senior government officials and generals siphoned off millions of American aid dollars into their own foreign bank accounts. Some generals created phantom military units on paper, then pocketed the pay allotted to nonexistent soldiers. For personal profit, government officials and army officers sold to the communists the very American ammunition and rifles given to help them fight the communists. Similarly, food and medicine intended for the Cambodian people were diverted into the black market or sold directly to the enemy. Peasants traveling to sell produce at markets had to pay bribes to military policemen in order to pass highway checkpoints. And the vigorously anticommunist newspaper *Damnoeng Pelprik* publicly complained about government forces looting peasant villages cleared of communists.

Given the popular perception of the two antagonists, the outcome of the war did not matter all that much to a people who comprehended only dimly, if at all, the ideological and political issues at stake. What did matter was that the war be ended. For most Cambodians had long been united in a profound craving for peace above all else. The fratricidal war had caused perhaps 600,000 deaths, and a majority of the dead were civilians lucklessly caught up in the crossfire between government and insurgent battalions or killed by bombings.* The war had disrupted the economy, ravaged the countryside, visited chaos on the cities, uprooted much of the population and generally benighted a serene little country, which by many standards was delightful.

Prior to 1970 Cambodian farmers without overly exerting themselves annually produced surpluses of rice. Land was plentiful, as were timber, cattle and poultry. The Mekong River, which flows by Phnom Penh, the Tonle Sap (Great Lake) and many lesser lakes about the capital teemed with fish. The people, urban and rural, were faithful, kindly believers in Theravada Buddhism and inheritors of a culture whose ancient grandeurs rivaled those of Greece, Rome or Egypt.

---

*Prince Norodom Sihanouk in October 1975 may have been the first to state that the war caused 600,000 deaths. He provided no explanation of the data or computations on which his statement was based. A number of Western journalists have reported that 600,000 deaths occurred without, however, adducing any basis for the figure except, in some cases, the statement of Prince Sihanouk. Still others have written that the war inflicted 600,000 "casualties," again without explaining the methods by which the toll was calculated.

The present Cambodian chief of state, Khieu Samphan, in August 1976 asserted that 1,000,000 people perished as a result of the war. He also failed to offer any basis for his figure.

The 1977 *World Almanac*, published by the Newspaper Enterprise Association of New York and Cleveland, states that "over

Phnom Penh was one of the most beguiling and friendly cities in all Asia, felicitously combining the distinctive charms of France and Cambodia. Wild guava trees topped by lush lavender foliage, beautiful flame trees adorned with huge red and yellow flowers and stately teak trees that yield wood hard enough to last 800 years lined the city's broad boulevards. Hibiscus, jasmine, dwarf pine and sweetly perfumed frangipani trees enhanced the many public and private gardens. Mediterranean and Oriental architecture blended colorfully in Parisian cafés, white colonial office buildings, Chinese shops, ornate pagodas, little frame houses standing on stilts near the river, neat brick homes in the heart of the city and grand villas on the outskirts. The central marketplace, a big open hall composed of four wings, symbolized the agricultural richness of the country. Housewives daily could choose from mountains of cucumbers, pumpkins, gourds, mangoes, papayas, sweet and white potatoes, carrots, onions, cabbage, tamarind leaves, water lilies, coconuts, succulent green oranges, jackfruit, lemons and watermelons. The market also abounded with pork, beef, chickens, ducks, trout, carp, sea crabs, field crabs, clams, oys-

---

100,000 died" during the war. No source of this figure is cited.

Various Western governmental and intelligence officials interviewed by the authors said that they lack reliable data which would enable them to calculate with any certainty the number who were killed and wounded. Several privately expressed doubts that either the Lon Nol government or the insurgents possessed the capability accurately to record the total number of military and civilian casualties suffered during a five-year war fought in jungles, on frequently fluid battlefields and on terrain that often changed hands.

ters, rice, noodles, fish paste, bean sprouts, eggs, herbs, spices and native candies.

Phnom Penh had been a city of tranquillity and orderliness, a city of gentle, laughing people, a city of striking women and good cuisine, a city of easy days and amiable nights. And it was the belief that the end of the war meant a return to such days and nights that inspired the spontaneous demonstrations the morning of April 17. The belief and desire were so strong that they overpowered reservations about the communists. Moreover, in that early-morning euphoria, apprehensions could be rationalized away.

Certainly, the communists would bring changes. They might punish, perhaps even kill, the "Seven Super Traitors," as they referred to leaders of the Lon Nol government. Others close to Lon Nol also might suffer. But toward the general populace the communists would be reasonable and just. They were, after all, fellow Khmers and fellow adherents of Buddhism, whose fundamental tenets include tolerance, respect and kindness toward others. One could accommodate to them, just as Cambodians always had accommodated to political change, just as the bamboo accommodates to shifting breezes.

Thus, the people who took to the streets to greet the communists looked on them not as conquerors but as heralds of peace, as augurs of a new era in which all could renew pursuit of the Khmer ideal, which is to "listen to the wind blow, watch the rice grow and make love."

The attitude of a twenty-three-year-old economics student, Ung Sok Choeu, probably typified the feelings of many in the welcoming crowds. Ung was the son of a wealthy family, and he certainly did not

consider himself personally deprived or oppressed.
Yet he was so disgusted with the war that he had
participated in student peace demonstrations which
were openly antigovernment and procommunist.
"That morning we were shouting, 'Victory! Victory!'
and I joined in with great glee. People were happy.
Life had been very difficult under Lon Nol. Not even
the middle classes, civil servants and university pro-
fessors managed to make ends meet anymore. Things
could only become better now. It wasn't that we loved
the Khmer Rouge so much, but seeing Lon Nol go was
worth an outburst of joy. After all, we were all
Khmers. What use was it that we should kill each
other?"

The statements of others who were there mirror
similar feelings. Banker Siv Hav: "We were happy to
see them [the communists]. It meant the war was
over." Pin-Sam Phon, supervisor of the city
waterworks: "The general reaction was that the Red
Khmers deserved their victory. Life in Phnom Penh
had become too hard to bear. There was corruption
everywhere. We wanted peace and had been wanting
it for a long time." A prosperous pharmacist, Kyheng
Savang: "The war was over; the Red Khmers had won;
celebrations were in order."

Throughout Cambodia the reactions were much the
same. A gem prospector from Pailin, Ngy Duch, remembers: "When we heard that Lon Nol's government had toppled, all of Pailin was happy. Villagers
near the city brought their drums outside their houses
and beat them; others played the flute; others sang
songs they improvised. The words the singers invented were that they were happy to welcome the Red
Khmers and that peace had finally come to their coun-

try. I was happy, too. I had been waiting for peace for a long time. It made me sad to see my compatriots get killed in a war without a purpose. I always thought that all those who fought in this war, on whatever side, were mad."

Phnom Penh residents looking for good omens in the initial actions of the occupation forces saw some. A communist officer riding in a jeep broadcast through a portable loudspeaker, "Brothers, fathers, sisters! Do not be afraid! The war is over!" When a squad approached a government armored personnel carrier deployed near the Catholic cathedral, the crew emerged and raised a white flag. A few of the conquerors hopped on the vehicle, and former enemies embraced, joked, laughed and slapped each other on the back. Refugees watching from the cathedral were elated. "Well, that was easy after all," one said. "The war is over! We are going home!" another exclaimed. Priests who witnessed the encounter also were encouraged.

Before communist troops reached the central market, government soldiers at about 7 A.M. began breaking into Chinese shops in the vicinity and murdered at least two shopkeepers who protested theft of their merchandise. The looting spread as civilians followed the example of the soldiers. The communists promptly ended the anarchy by announcing through their loudspeakers that all looters would be summarily shot or hanged.

At the same time, though, there were early portents troublesome even to optimistic onlookers. Despite some individual gestures of cordiality, most of the occupation troops did not deign to acknowledge, much less return, the exuberant greetings offered

them. The welcoming cheers, the cries of peace had
no more visible effect on them than they would have
had on robots. As the arriving communist columns
lengthened and the dark little figures proliferated in
the blinding morning sunlight, their studied silence,
broken only by the loudspeakers, seemed contemptuous and threatening.

Virtually all government soldiers quickly obeyed
communist commands to lay down their arms. Upon
gathering up the surrendered weapons, the communists subjected groups of soldiers to an extreme
Oriental humiliation by forcing them to shed their
boots and uniforms and march off in their underwear.

Although occupation authorities resolutely
stopped looting by civilians and government soldiers, they did nothing to deter wholesale looting by
their own troops. Soon communist soldiers rampaged
through commercial districts, shooting open the
bolted doors of shops or ripping them off with ropes
attached to jeeps. Ball-point pens, jewelry, watches,
particularly Omega watches, liquor, anything with
wheels or anything exotic attracted them most.
Bizarre scenes developed as they enjoyed the booty.

A beaming guerrilla strolled by the French embassy
attired in a long crimson woolen overcoat, an incon-
gruous addition to his foreboding black uniform. In
an emergency operating theater established by a Scot-
tish medical team at Hotel Le Phnom, physicians
watched in dismay as troops burst in and, finding no
liquor, swigged down the contents of serum bottles.
Many of the soldiers had never driven vehicles, or
their driving skills had atrophied in the jungles, and
they tumbled off motorcycles or crashed them into
trees. Newly liberated cars careered down the streets,

swerving into each other and sometimes smashing into storefronts. At the Olympic Market a jeep loaded with ammunition crashed into a utility pole, exploded and disappeared in flames. Unable to start a stolen Honda, a frustrated young communist riddled it with bullets. Others vented their wrath on stalled automobiles by stomping on the hoods or slashing the tires.

By 8:30 A.M. communist troops were halting traffic to confiscate cars, motorcycles and bicycles. During these robberies the soldiers habitually invoked the strange term *Angka Loeu*. Literally, *Angka* (Organization) and *Loeu* (Higher) translate into English as the Higher Organization, but a better rendition of the term's meaning probably would be the Organization on High. With a politeness belied by pointed rifles or pistols, the communists would say: "*Angka Loeu* proposes that you lend me your motorcycle.... *Angka Loeu* proposes that you drive me.... "

Some refugees from communist-occupied areas had heard and learned to dread the term. They knew that *Angka Loeu* exercised omnipotence over all communist soldiers and commissars and that "We are sending you to *Angka Loeu*" or "*Angka Loeu* wants to reeducate you" was a euphemism for the death sentence. However, most people in Phnom Penh never had heard of *Angka Loeu*, and its mysterious, faceless connotation was compounded in their eyes by the awe and unquestioning obedience it commanded among the communist troops. Nobody knew exactly what or where *Angka Loeu* was. Soon everybody would discover that it was everywhere.

Shortly after the first robberies, the killing began. An eighteen-year-old high-school student, Sar Sam, saw it start. "At eight forty-five that morning a Red Khmer killed Mr. Kim, our neighbor. Mr. Kim was about forty-two. He joined the army in 1971 as a private second class, and he had only one leg. He lived about eighteen meters from us, and he was killed in his house. I saw one Red Khmer, with fixed bayonet, enter Mr. Kim's house and leave it again. Together with lots of other people, I entered Mr. Kim's house to see what had happened. Mr. Kim, wearing his military uniform, was lying on the tiled floor, a wound in his belly. He was dead. Everybody was sad, and nobody said a word. I thought the Red Khmer had killed him because he did not go out to welcome them and also because he was a military.

"At about eight fifty I saw another Red Khmer kill a man of about fifty whom I did not know. The man had been wounded by a shell during the night, and although he was hit in the head, he was still alive. His family had brought him outside their house because they were trying to find somebody who would take him to the hospital. But at eight fifty a Red Khmer killed him with an American AR-15 rifle. He was about eighteen and said that it was impossible to survive with the kind of head injury the man had got."

About the same time ten to twenty civil servants and soldiers walked out of a government building. Waiting communist troops, without warning or explanation, cut them down with machine-gun fire. Later, in front of the Ministry of Information, communist soldiers surrounded a man who, by some word or gesture, had given offense and kicked and stabbed him. The crowd watched as he slowly died.

Still, there were grounds for hope. Through the centuries other armies in other places doubtless had

done the same as the communists did during their
first few hours in Phnom Penh. Many of the occupation troops must have been physically and psychologically fatigued by privations of the jungle and
tensions of battle. Many were intoxicated, if not by
quaffs of alcohol, then by victory. Many had never
seen a city before, and perhaps they were further
intoxicated by the dazzling sights of a city which they
had been taught, both by their rural background and
communist indoctrination, to think of as a sink of
iniquity. Many were little more than children who
had been trained in little other than killing.
Scattering quickly through strange streets, many of
the troops in the initial chaos undoubtedly were
beyond the reach of orders or communications from
their commanders. Thus, it is possible that the early
killing and looting represented not the policies of
Angka Loeu but the aberrations of individual
soldiers.

However, there can be no argument about what
began between 9 and 10 A.M. It was clearly and coldly
premeditated by *Angka Loeu*. And modern history
fails to show that anything quite like it ever has happened before.

At about 9 A.M. in his private clinic across the street
from the Military Hospital, Dr. Vann Hay was attend-
ing a colonel wounded in the last hours of the bombardment. "I was still in the operating room when I
was told that Red Khmer soldiers were at the door of
the clinic asking that everybody leave immediately.
As soon as I had finished with the colonel, I went to
talk to the Red Khmers. There were maybe twenty of
them, all very young, and they repeated their order.
" 'These people here have been hospitalized be-

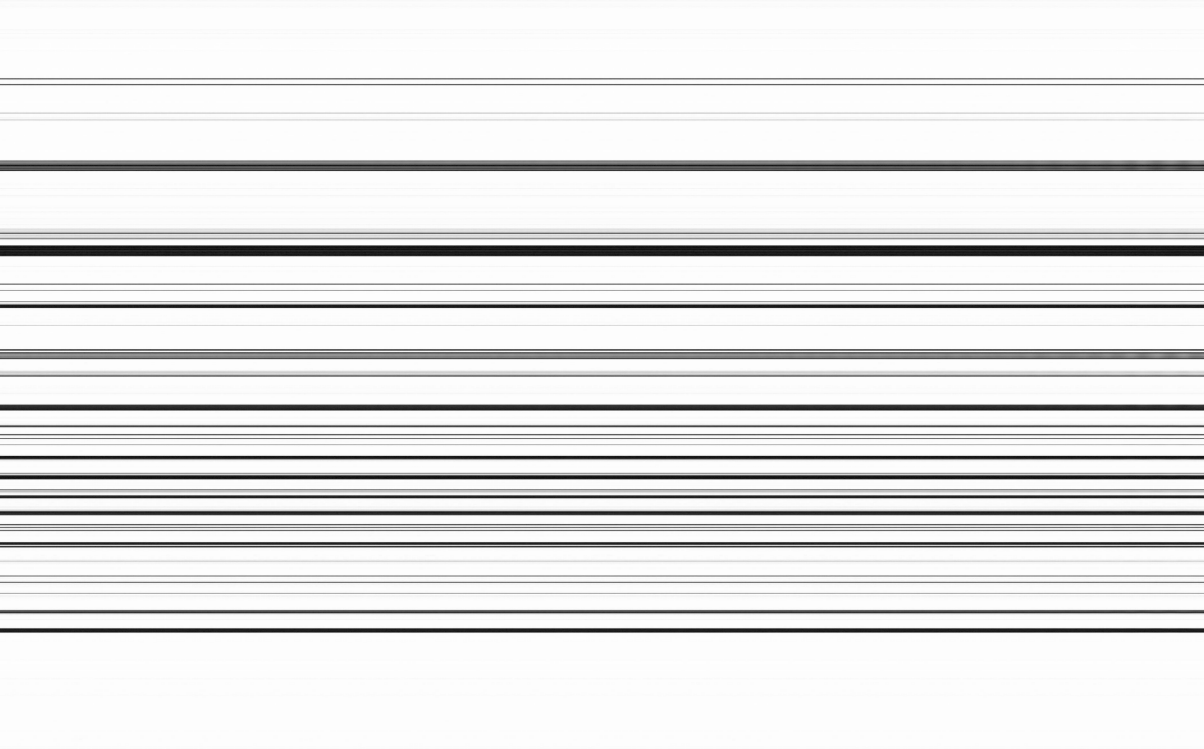

Shooting in

loudspeakers, ba n

harshly, sometim

tesy, troops in the

the same astonis

Every man, wom

occupation, back

must get out of

families to depart

while others told

or until the next d

would be away for

others said for thr

period of time.''

whatever belongin

them they should

would provide for

instructed to mar

rections or along

ways for distance

apparently, was to

he reached his va

To those who as

homes and city, co

explanations: ''I

bomb.'' . . . ''The

still corrupting for

have to clean out t

three days so we ca

don't know; it's ju

explanation which

the most valid

Catholic priests by

''From now on, if

out and work in the rice paddies. They should learn
that their lives depend on a grain of rice. Plowing the
soil, planting and harvesting rice will teach them the
real value of things. Cities are evil. There are money
and trade in cities, and both have a corrupting influence. People are good, but cities are evil. That is why
we shall do away with cities."

Inexplicably, the communists concentrated initially upon expelling the sick and wounded from
hospitals which were jammed with fresh casualties of
the last bombardment. Troops stormed into the Preah
Ket Melea Hospital, Phnom Penh's largest and oldest,
and shouted to patients, physicians and nurses alike,
"Out! Everybody out! Get out!" They made no distinction between bedridden and ambulatory patients,
between the convalescing and the dying, between
those awaiting surgery and those who had just undergone surgery. Hundreds of men, women and children
in pajamas limped, hobbled, struggled out of the hospital into the streets where the midday sun had raised
the temperature to well over 100 degrees Fahrenheit.
Relatives or friends pushed the beds of patients too
wounded, crippled or enfeebled to walk, some holding aloft perfusion bottles dripping plasma or serum
into the bodies of loved ones. One man carried his
son, whose legs had just been amputated. The ban-
dages on both stumps were red with blood, and the
son, who appeared to be about twenty-two, was
screaming, "You can't leave me like this! Kill me!
Please kill me!"

Reporting for training duty at Borei Keila Hospital,
Kem Phaly, a twenty-one-year-old medical student,
saw troops routing doctors and nurses at gunpoint.
Running through wards brandishing rifles, they

shouted, "Everyone out! Out of the hospital, out of the city! We have to search for CIA agents!" The soldiers swept through the hospital so quickly that they inadvertently left behind some patients who were too sick to move. And Kem Phaly, along with one physician and two nurses, evaded the evacuation order by disguising themselves as such patients.

However, other hospitals were emptied totally, with the beds of those too sick to move simply being shoved into the streets. Friendless, dying patients thus ousted did the best they could. Two very sick men who had no one to help them got into one bed and labored to propel themselves down the street with sticks, as if punting.

While herding everyone out of public hospitals, bands of soldiers also emptied private clinics and homes for invalids. Accompanied by a fellow university student, Prach Chhea at about 11 A.M. went to visit his crippled brother who lived near the Royal Palace in a barracks set aside for disabled war veterans and their families. "I took the street along the Mekong until I arrived in front of my brother's barracks. There was utter havoc. Shooting and cries could be heard from inside the building. Women and children were running out of the door, and Red Khmer soldiers were coming in and out. My friend and I were frightened. 'They are shooting the invalids! Disaster has struck!' I said to my friend....

"There was no way on earth we could find my brother, so we went by motorcycle to the Military Hospital, where we witnessed a similar scene. Shots resounded from within, while families hastily were pushing hospital patients out of the building on beds and wheeled stretchers. People were in such a hurry to get out that they were shoving and pushing each other, and some of the sick men who had fallen to the ground were crying out with pain. We didn't want to stay and watch anymore."

Shortly before noon a noted French scholar, Father François Ponchaud, looked out from behind shutters of the Catholic Mission and saw an agonized procession of several hundred hospital patients slowly wending their way out of the city toward the unknown. Many wore casts; many walked on crutches; virtually all were in pajamas. Quite a few lay in beds or on stretchers pushed or carried by relatives. Again, above some patients, friends or relatives held perfusion bottles, determined to sustain life as long as possible.

Similar processions were seen by countless thousands of Cambodians, as well as by numerous foreigners of diverse nationalities. One trained observer who watched them from the French embassy compound was Jon Swain, a twenty-seven-year-old British journalist who had spent much of his career in Indochina. Although not procommunist, Swain, like many other Western reporters, was personally contemptuous of the Lon Nol regime and not entirely unsympathetic to the cause of the insurgents. In daring quests for authentic stories he had established a reputation for extreme bravery, and he had seen the worst of the war. Nothing, though, prepared him for what he saw on April 17. Recording the scenes in his diary as they unfolded, he wrote that the communists were "tipping out patients like garbage into the streets. . . .

"Bandaged men and women hobble by the embassy. Wives push wounded soldier husbands on hospital beds on wheels, some with serum drips still attached. In five years of war, this is the greatest caravan of human misery I have seen.

"The Khmer Rouge must know that few of the city's 20,000 wounded will survive. One can only conclude that they have no humanitarian instincts. The entire city is being emptied of its people: the old, the sick, the infirm, the hungry, the orphans, without exception."

From noon onward the masses in the streets multiplied as communist troops uprooted more and more families. In the ever-thickening congestion, movement became progressively difficult. Along some boulevards families advanced no more than 180 meters an hour, and driving became impossible. So people pushed cars, motorcycles, bicycles and a motley assortment of carts, loaded with whatever they had been able to assemble in haste and uncertainty—rice, canned food, pots, pans, clothes, blankets, live chickens, family treasures, condensed milk for babies. People without vehicles carried bundles of belongings in their arms and on their shoulders, and many also bore human cargoes—fearful, fretting children, aged or sick relatives too weak to walk.

That same afternoon the communists began to purge the capital of all literature, all printed matter. Rare and ancient manuscripts from temples and museums; the records of government and business; the libraries of schools, universities, hospitals and private residences; dictionaries, medical textbooks, any bound volume, any periodical regardless of content, regardless of where found—all were targets.

Troops ransacked the Royal Palace, government

ministries and commercial offices, indiscriminately
flinging documents and papers into the streets. Opposite the palace they burned down an entire
bookstore. Tens of thousands, perhaps hundreds of
thousands, of books were thrown into the Mekong or
burned on the riverbanks. At the Soviet Hospital (so
named because it was built with Russian aid), soldiers
gathered up all books and magazines, including the
medical library, and carted them to a nearby shed.
Setting the shed afire with gasoline, they ignited a
conflagration that for a while endangered the hospital
itself. Untold numbers of books were burned at a city
dump some 5 kilometers from the hospital, and the
libraries of Phnom Penh University and Buddhist
University went up in flames.

The director of the Banque Khmer de Commerce sat
quietly in his office waiting to give Cambodia's new
rulers the keys to the vaults. Suddenly troops
swarmed into the office, hustled him outside, then
methodically plundered the bank. But rather than
steal money, they burned it by the millions of riels
(the Cambodian currency unit). From other re-
positories, troops scooped up banknotes and stuffed
them into rice sacks, which they tossed into the
streets for destruction along with books.
Additionally, they simply threw away so much
money that at times banknotes fluttered through the
streets like ticker tape.

While routing people from their homes, soldiers
frequently overturned furniture and cabinets,
smashed glassware and crockery, ripped up bedding
and generally devastated the interior. In many cases
they flung contents of houses into the street to be
burned or ruined by the weather.

People not yet visited by communist squads hid in their homes, and families—husbands, wives, children, grandparents, brothers, sisters, uncles, aunts, nieces, nephews, distant cousins—gathered to confront the crisis together. While some discussed how they should prepare for the worst, others tried to reject the import of all that was visible in the streets. Everyone, in the homes and streets, hungered for an authoritative explanation that would tell them, if not what they wanted to hear, then at least what actually was happening and what was to happen.

Hence everybody listened intently when, shortly before 1 P.M., Radio Phnom Penh broadcast a recorded message from the assistant chief of staff, General Mey Sichan. The war was lost, he sadly announced. While the tape played on, a communist detachment seized the radio station and rushed into the studio. Just as the general's choked voice informed listeners that the government soon would "make a decision with a delegation of our brothers of the other side about a way to bring peace," another voice terminated the broadcast: "We do not want negotiations; rather, to take the capital by force." Then Radio Phnom Penh went off the air again.

The soldiers came after Ang Sokthan and her family in midafternoon. Ang was a bright, pretty girl of twenty-two with a quick, natural smile that made others smile. Though her parents were poor farmers near the provincial capital of Siem Reap, they helped all their children acquire an education, and Ang was in her third year of pharmacy studies at Phnom Penh University. Like most young people, she had cheered the communist troops entering the city. "We raised white sheets to welcome them and to express our faithfulness to them. Every one of us hoped that from now on we would live in peace and be free from war." But when the troops began shooting and looting, she fled in fright to the large three-story house of her cousin, a dentist, who lived in the O Russey section half a kilometer southwest of the central market. Three families, comprising thirty-one people all related in one way or another, had assembled at the house. Among them were Ang's sister, Anna, nineteen, and two of her brothers, Kim, twenty-five, and Tam, twenty-three, both of whom were suffering from hepatitis.

Ang asked the group of soldiers who ordered them out of the city where they should go. "Anywhere; as far away as possible," one replied. Asked how long they would have to stay away, the soldier answered only, "For a period of time."

The three families departed at 5 P.M. "I had only one dress and no food with me, no rice, no cooking utensils. We took money, but the Khmer Rouge soon made us throw it away. One of my relatives, the dentist's wife, was pregnant; the baby was due any day, but she still had to go. She packed some cans of condensed milk in case the child came early while we were on the road. We brought some blankets, some small pillows for the baby, mosquito nets and cookies for the children in case they cried.

"On the road we took toward Stoeng Meanchey, there was a huge crowd of people of every age and every condition, including young, old and sick. Some people carried their belongings on their heads, their shoulders and their hips. They carried live ducks trussed up and pigs tied like dogs with leashes and led along the road. Some could barely walk. Some just dragged each other. I remember a two-deck bed being pushed by a family. There were two women in it, one of whom had just given birth. For some of the aged, families had improvised slings—a pole held by two people with three pieces of rope coming down from the center to a circular seat. Other old people were being carried in makeshift hammocks across relatives' shoulders.

"They traveled in groups, family by family. Parents walked slowly, tightly holding the hands of their children. The children, some with their hands clinging to their parents' belts or clothes, some crying and some not; all looked terrified. One could get lost from the others easily if they were separated just a few meters apart. And if lost from each other, they would have very little chance of finding each other again. There were many children who were lost, and they were miserable."

It was dusk when a communist patrol halted the party and approached Kim, who was pushing his motorcycle. "*Angka Loeu* offers to borrow this motorcycle," a soldier said politely. With equal politeness, Kim declined the offer.

Raising his rifle, a soldier yelled, "Don't make us do it," and Kim gave up his motorcycle.

Through tears, Ang looked back at the flames shooting up from bonfires in which books and documents were being burned. "I seemed suddenly to know that I would never again see my home or my parents." Her premonition was correct. But for all her prescience she could not have imagined the horror that awaited her in the next months or the reservoir of courage that would enable her to survive and surmount it.

The streams of benumbed and bewildered unfortunates trudging out of the city steadily swelled through the afternoon, and that evening probably several hundred thousand people slept by the streets or roads. Nevertheless, the majority of residents managed to stay in their homes during the first night of the occupation. Probably fewer than 10,000 communist troops had invaded the city, and these were insufficient in the first hours to tell, much less compel, all 3,000,000 inhabitants to get out. Moreover, the differing orders which forced some families to leave instantly while permitting others to stay a few hours more reflected some confusion among the troops about how quickly the city was to be denuded of its citizens. But early the next morning, roughly twenty-four hours after the advent of peace, the communists began routing out the people much more methodically and vigorously.

After soldiers closed his clinic, Dr. Vann Hay hurried home. "Group after group of Red Khmers came to the house all day long. Some said we had to leave right away, others that we could stay on until the next day. Their orders always came from *Angka Loeu*, which seemed to be their superiors. I had never heard the word before.

"On April 18, early in the morning, one of the groups which had come by the day before reappeared. 'Leave immediately, or we will shoot all of you,' one said. I put my father-in-law into the car, and we left. The streets were packed with people, all heading toward the outskirts. It was like a river swelling constantly and regularly, dragging everybody along.

"*Angka Loeu* seemed omnipresent. Always *Angka Loeu* was giving new orders. And the Red Khmers seemed to execute all *Angka Loeu* orders without blinking an eye. I couldn't understand how anything as anonymous as *Angka Loeu* could bring forth such blind obedience."

In the name of *Angka*, parties of four to six soldiers systematically went from door to door, repeating the same order, and by midmorning the streets teemed with hundreds of thousands of people. Among the driven multitudes a new realization soon spread: Each soldier servant of *Angka* held death at his or her fingertips, and to disobey *Angka* or displease its servants invited instant death.

Given the alternative of leaving or being shot, Dost Mohammed, an electronics salesman, departed on the morning of the eighteenth with his wife, six children and his mother. They placed his mother, who was seventy-five and dying, on a bicycle which Dost and his son pushed. Some traffic was still moving on the street along which they walked, and a pedicab rolled past them. "Don't go on that side of the road!" a soldier shouted at the driver. The pedicab did not alter course, so a soldier killed the driver with machine-gun fire. Another soldier riddled the driver of a Datsun who failed to heed, perhaps even hear, an order to halt. A man driving a Chevrolet ignored one order but complied with a second command to stop. A young soldier thrust his rifle through the window of the car, then shot the driver through the heart, and he crumpled in the arms of his wife, sitting in the front passenger seat. Racing to find his family before leaving the city, a man pedaled his bicycle into a street the communists had closed near the O Russey section. "I'm going to pick up my family," he yelled to guards. Without warning, a soldier sprayed him with machine-gun bullets, and he fell to the street dead.

The communists routinely used rockets and bazookas to blast the recalcitrant out of their houses. Having ordered all villas in the fashionable Boulevard Monivong vacated, troops detected movement behind the window of one of the large houses. They fired a bazooka round into a window, and eight occupants ran in panic out the front door. Soldiers lined them all up—three men, three women and two children—and shot each. The dead were servants and their families. Before their employer had left on a trip abroad, they had promised to guard the house by remaining in it no matter what happened.

The driven masses also quickly learned that *Angka* tolerated no demands, protests or other troublemaking. Ousted from their homes the morning of the eighteenth, two men got into a fight on the street. Soldiers promptly settled the dispute by killing both. On Monivong Bridge soldiers took a young man prisoner and bound his hands behind his back, possibly because he wore long hair. He seemed to have been in the tropical sun for some time, and he pleaded for water.

"We don't have any," a soldier told him.

"If you don't give me water," cried the youth, "then kill me!" A soldier calmly aimed his rifle, killed him and dumped the body off the bridge into the Bassac River.

Lost children, thirsty and hungry, helpless and hopeless, were among the more pitiable sights of the evacuation. Without the protection and nourishment afforded by parents, they would be among the first to perish. So in the crush of the crowds, parents clung tightly and desperately to their small children.

Near the French embassy a French schoolteacher

observed a communist patrol march from an alley
through a line of refugees and by happenstance part a
mother and father from their children. The frantic
parents protested and sought to reclaim their children, now on the other side of the communist column.
The patrol leader thereupon fired a volley of rifle
shots, killing both mother and father.

Although not everybody personally witnessed
such summary executions, virtually everybody saw
the consequences of them in the form of the corpses of
men, women and children rapidly bloating and rotting in the hot sun. The bodies, sometimes grotesquely contorted in agony, yielded a nauseating, pervasive stench, and they had a transfiguring effect on
the hundreds of thousands of people being exiled.
Almost overnight Phnom Penh residents, who had
been known for their spontaneity and gaiety, their
uninhibited curiosity and friendliness, became a silent, cowed herd fearful of speaking to one another or
doing anything which might single them out for the
attention of *Angka*.

Whether by design or by negligence, *Angka* on the
evening of the eighteenth allowed the water supply to
cease throughout the city. Most families had brought
along some food, but not water, and its sudden un-
availability caused measureless suffering. People
were reduced to drinking from ponds in parks and
gardens, from private swimming pools, from stagnant
puddles. Even these sources swiftly dwindled, and if
trapped in the interior of crowds, people had difficulty fighting their way to them whenever they were
sighted. The lack of potable water created dysentery,
resulting in dehydration, a killer that was to treat the
people as mercilessly as *Angka* itself throughout the
great exodus. By the third day of the evacuation,

Saturday, the nineteenth, some of the very young, the very old and the very sick began to die of this and other simple afflictions such as exposure and malnutrition. Deaths during childbirth on the streets also were frequent.

Ly Bun Heng, one of Phnom Penh's leading architects, who cut short a stay in Paris and flew back to welcome the communists, remembers: "On Boulevard Monivong I saw two women giving birth amid the crowd of camping refugees. One was in the back seat of a Volkswagen in what looked like the most uncomfortable position. The other was on the sidewalk under a tamarind tree, maybe fourteen meters from my house. She was lying on a piece of cloth, shouting, 'Help! Help me!'

"Her husband was pushing through the crowd, calling for a doctor. Women had formed a circle around the future mother, holding out their skirts sideways to shield her from the crowd. It was a pitiful sight. So I went up to my house and yelled for the leader of the Red Khmers.

"'I have three bedrooms next to my garage,' I said. 'They are not locked. Please let us have one so this lady can have her baby in more decent conditions.'

"They got furious. 'Go away and don't come back,' the chief shouted. 'Don't bother us.'

"I went back to the woman, who meanwhile was about to have her baby. Hordes of curious children tried to get a look at the scene. I chased them away, and they made a lot of noise. Meanwhile, the baby was born, and one woman said, 'We must cut the umbilical cord.'

"Everybody began to shout at once. 'Cut what?' 'Where does it have to be cut?'

"Hearing all the racket, the Khmer Rouge chief

came out and yelled, 'Gatherings are forbidden! Disperse! Disperse!' But in all the noise the people didn't hear, so the soldier whipped out a pistol and began shooting into the tamarind tree. A shower of leaves fell upon the woman and the newborn baby. It was all like a nightmare.''

Along the principal boulevards leading to the national highways out of Phnom Penh, the sheer magnitude of the throngs was such that people progressed only a short distance every twenty-four hours. It took Thach Bun Rath, an eighteen-year-old business school student, three days to walk approximately 4 kilometers from his home to the Monivong Bridge. "The heat was intense, and people were dying in the streets. I saw the bodies of a number of old people by the wayside, and others who were in agony. A young woman was carrying a dead baby in her arms. She was crying silently because she did not want to attract the Red Khmers' attention, and she did not want to leave the tiny body on the street.

"Some of the many bodies were people who had been shot. Not just military, but women and children as well. I had no luggage with me, neither food nor water, so I had to beg to survive.''

Ea Than, a twenty-seven-year-old unmarried librarian, left his home on the eighteenth in a family party composed of his parents, brothers, sisters, uncles and aunts—about a dozen people.

"Early in the morning my family and I prepared our luggage—clothes, food, cooking gear—and we heaped most of this onto my father's bicycle. The Khmer Rouge were pushing us on, shouting, 'Go on! Move on!' as soon as we left the house. I asked one of them where we were supposed to go.

" 'Don't worry, you'll see all right. Everybody has to leave town for three days so we can clean it up. Just follow the crowd,' he said.

"And a huge crowd there was. We were slowly moving south, along Boulevard Mao Tse-tung. The Khmer Rouge were lining the street, and nobody was allowed to turn back. I heard somebody in the crowd tell how a doctor had been chased from his office. When he said he wanted to go back in to change his smock, the Red Khmers shot him.

"All of Phnom Penh seemed to be leaving toward the south. We were packed like sardines, and progress was unbelievably slow. It took us three days and three nights to cover the three kilometers between our house and Monivong Bridge [the bridge across the Bassac was a major exit from Phnom Penh]. Rumors were being passed along all the way. One was that *Angka* wanted us to walk to Takhmau [a city south of the capital]; another that *Angka* had given orders we should march to the Vietnamese border to defend our country. I had heard about *Angka* during the war already. It used to be a terrifying word. I knew that all those who were against the Red Khmers would be sent to *Angka Loeu*. Everything coming from *Angka* seemed frightening, particularly the order to walk all the way to the border. The crowd and myself were scared. There was no place to take shelter from the scorching sun. We were advancing one kilometer every twenty-four hours. How long would it take us to reach the border? How many of us would survive even the march to Takhmau?

"Rotting bodies of soldiers and civilians were lining the streets, some of them with their mouths wide open and crawling with worms. There was nobody to bury them, and the smell in the heat was sickening. But the Red Khmers did not seem bothered. They sometimes sat right next to a body to eat their rice.

"At one point walking next to me was a woman of about thirty, a baby in one arm, holding the hand of a boy of about four with the other. There was a look of utter despair on her face. Then she walked to the side of the street and gently put her baby on a tuft of grass. It was dead. Nobody seemed to have any tears to cry.

"All the way the Red Khmers were shooting into the air and at houses by the streets. 'Go on! Move on!' they shouted.

"At the speed we were going, nobody had enough food for the long march. I asked one of the Red Khmer soldiers, 'How are we going to survive with the little food all of us have brought?'

"'That means you will have to walk faster to reach *Angka*. *Angka* will give you food,' he replied.

"Near the Monivong Bridge were still more rotting bodies. I wondered for how long they had been there, exposed to the sun. Obviously, everybody was being chased from Phnom Penh, even the bonzes and the sick. Hospital beds were being pushed by families. Those who had no family tried to move on their own.

"By that time nobody showed any reactions to anything anymore. We simply followed each other like cattle. All courtesy, all respect of hierarchy had vanished. It was every man for himself, with only one idea: how to survive."

While the vast masses slowly passed, Tevi Rosa hid with her mother and relatives in a splendid white villa on Boulevard Monivong. Rosa was one of those children equally beautiful in spirit, manner and body. At fourteen, she looked like a fully matured and fortunately endowed woman with dark eyes, long raven hair and a flawless apricot-colored complexion. She spoke with a soft voice whose diction was born of her cultured home and education at the French Lycée Descartes. Her father was a romantic, handsome colonel in the army, and her mother was a lovely sister of architect Ly Bun Heng. From her mother, Rosa had inherited deep faith in Buddhism and through it acquired inner serenity and the habit of kindness toward all.

As Phnom Penh fell, Rosa's father took his wife and their five children to Ly's villa and entrusted them to his care. He hugged Rosa and said, "I will not be seeing you for some time." Then he drove off in the jeep she knew well.

There were about twenty people in the villa, including Ly's nine relatives, servants and their families. Soldiers ordered all to leave on the eighteenth, but thinking the order was unauthorized or surely would be rescinded, they closed the shutters and stayed. The next day more soldiers told them to get out. Pointing to the jammed streets, Ly persuaded them it would be futile to depart for the moment and let them rest on cots in the garden. The exhausted young soldiers fell into a long sleep and thereby inadvertently afforded a kind of protection to the house. But later that morning three older, harder soldiers were outraged to find the villa still occupied. "You will explain to *Angka Loeu*," the leader announced. Their hands tied behind them, Ly and his brother were shoved from the villa with rifles in their backs. Rosa and her mother cried uncontrollably, certain that both were doomed.

Ly, though, was a worldly, keen, quick-witted man

whose self-confidence at times approached impudent foolhardiness, and he was not paralyzed by the specter of *Angka Loeu*. By persuasively explaining his personal ties to a number of prominent men who had fought Lon Nol, he ultimately convinced his interrogators that he was their innocent sympathizer. They released him and his brother and even allowed them time to load belongings into his red Fiat before forsaking the villa.

While Ly steered and his elderly father rode in the car, Rosa and the rest of the family pushed it down the jammed boulevard all afternoon. By nightfall they had arrived at the Law School of Phnom Penh University—540 meters from the villa. Because the principal thoroughfares out of the city could not accommodate any more people, the communists allowed refugees temporarily to camp at the school. Rosa and her family slept that night on mats among thousands of others, unable to comprehend but now too afraid to ask why they could not sleep in their own beds 540 meters away.

The lack of water, the excrement, the suffocating congestion, the relentless heat and pervasive anxiety made conditions at the encampment squalid. Rosa remembers: "A man nearby had a hysterical outburst. He screamed, 'It's impossible to live like this, like cattle. I don't want any more of this; it is too hard, too inhuman.' That evening a Red Khmer appeared and told the man, 'Come with me to *Angka Loeu*.'

"The man never came back. We knew from the government militaries who used to come to our house that *Angka Loeu* was a place of no return, that it was the place where the Red Khmers killed people. So we knew the man would never come back."

Troops early in the afternoon of April 23 peppered the sky with rifle and machine-gun fire by way of advising all at the Law School that their time had come. The mobs on the boulevards had sufficiently thinned to allow one to walk normally, if slowly. With the family pushing the car, Ly tried to take a route toward Vietnam. They had gone only about 450 meters when a patrol stopped and searched the car, hunting for jewelry, radios, ball-point pens and watches. Ly had concealed all valuables under the seats, so the soldiers confiscated only a flashlight.

As darkness descended, Ly spotted what appeared to be an empty house. Instead of sleeping on the roadsides, ditches or fields as most evacuees had to do, he led the family into it for the night. "What a funny smell in this house!" Rosa exclaimed.

"Probably just dead rats and mice," Ly assured her.

In the morning they found under a bed the body of a man lying in a splotch of dried blood. He had been bayoneted to death. Another body lay in an adjoining room, and a third behind the house. The body of a woman, who had been shot in the back, was huddled by the kitchen stove. A pot of water and rice was in front of her, and Ly concluded she probably had been killed while preparing family dinner.

The streets now were so relatively clear that the family reached the outskirts of the city that day. Rosa doubtless will never forget the last sights. "Just as we left Phnom Penh, we passed a dozen or more bodies. They were lying by the roadside, already swollen and their clothes rotting. I couldn't see whether they wore uniforms or not because I could barely stand the sight of them. I'm sure they had been shot, for they were all crumpled up. They weren't stretched out peacefully

as the body of someone who died a natural death
would be. The strong stench made me nauseated and
dizzy. In normal times I would have cried, but then I
just couldn't. No tears would come. Even Mummy,
who cries for the smallest little things, was unable to
cry. I felt deeply sorry for the people who had died.
My mother kept saying, 'Poor people! Poor people!' "

Rosa had always been a child who grieved at injury
to any living being. What lay ahead was to transform
her into a traumatized woman willing to kill.

Having drained virtually all life out of Phnom
Penh, the communists, by April 23, had commenced
emptying the other principal cities of Cambodia.*
Because the populations were much smaller and thus
much more manageable, it appears that troops were
able to evacuate completely most of the provincial
cities in less than twenty-four hours.† Nevertheless,
in the provinces the scenes and agonies of Phnom
Penh were duplicated, albeit on a lesser scale and in a
shorter time.

In Battambang, truck driver Ma Chheang saw
black-clad soldiers shoot to death an entire family
that failed instantly to obey the evacuation order.
Among the slain was a baby. Nuom Linna, a twenty-
three-year-old student, saw *Angka* riflemen cut down

---

*The cities and their estimated populations were: Battambang
200,000; Svay Rieng, 130,000; Kompong Chhnang 60,000; Kompong Speu 60,000; Kompong Cham 40,000; Pailin 40,000; Siem
Reap 50,000; Pursat 40,000; Kampot 40,000; Takeo 40,000; Kompong Som 25,000; Poipet 20,000; and Sisophon 15,000.

†Eyewitness accounts from some of the smaller cities are lacking. However, according to eyewitnesses, the communists succeeded in expelling everyone from the largest provincial city,
Battambang, in about fifteen hours and several of the smaller
cities in less time.

three men who tried to go home and collect belongings before joining the exodus. For unexplained reasons, the communists even before the evacuation killed a much-beloved physician, Colonel Tan Pok, chief of Military Hospital 403 in Battambang. Here, as in Phnom Penh and other cities, troops also wantonly destroyed books, furniture, automobiles, motorcycles and other valuables they themselves might have put to good use. To awed onlookers, soldiers sometimes explained that they were "cleansing" or "cleaning out" the cities. One boasted, "We shall turn the cities into countrysides and the countryside into cities."

In Siem Reap frenzied troops ravaged civilian and military hospitals, slaughtering patients in their beds, smashing medical equipment and wrecking operating rooms. With clubs, knives and bullets, they massacred approximately 100 patients, including women recuperating from childbirth, at the civilian Monte Peth Hospital and murdered about 40 patients at Military Hospital 404.

In Pailin, Ngy Duch, the young gem prospector who had played his flute to celebrate peace, watched transfixed as troops lined up three young men and two girls against a pagoda wall. Machine guns stuttered, and the five fell lifelessly forward on the street. "They will kill us all," screamed Ngy's elderly mother. Like animals before a wildfire, Ngy, his mother and all around fled.

The pattern was similar almost everywhere. Suddenly portable loudspeakers blared the astonishing order to leave. Suddenly families were forced to give up their homes and the possessions of a lifetime to march toward the jungles and a fate nobody would explain. The suddenness of the orders, the necessity

to comply immediately or die often separated husbands from wives, children from parents. Relatives
tacked notes on trees reporting the direction in which
they had departed, hoping that loved ones by chance
might see and be able to follow. The stronger helped
or carried the weaker, and the weakest soon started to
die.

The American bombers of which *Angka Loeu*
warned the people never appeared. But on April 18 an
American F-4 Phantom outfitted for reconnaissance
recorded the beginning of the exodus from Phnom
Penh. Its photographs showed the long antlike lines
of human beings jamming the streets and stretching
into the countryside. Later in April another American
reconnaissance plane repeatedly circled the skies
above Phnom Penh. Its cameras could detect almost
no signs of life of any kind.

Phnom Penh, a city of more than 3,000,000 people,
had been transformed into a vast, still wasteland occupied primarily by corpses, stray dogs, pigs, ducks,
chickens and *Angka Loeu* patrols standing guard to
ensure that human life did not return. Around the
Soviet Hospital lay the remains of nonambulatory
patients who had been dumped on the grounds and
who had had no friends to take them away before
death did so. A few dying souls were propped up
against the wall outside, deposited there by relatives
who prayed that somebody might help them.
Stretched out at the edge of architect Ly's swimming
pool was the body of a white-haired woman, her hand
reaching with a cup for water. Desolate streets were
cluttered with broken furniture, crockery, burst cush-
ions, clothing and the little inconsequential treasures
of vanished families. At Phnom Penh University pigs,

hens and ducks rooted and pecked around classrooms; rice and banana trees had been planted over a large area of the campus. The most important university in Cambodia now was a farm. In large sectors of the city not a human voice could be heard. Open doors of empty, looted houses creaked, and banknotes or documents littering the streets rustled in the wind; occasionally a starving dog barked forlornly; now and then a pedicab creaked by loaded with bodies to be dumped in the river. Otherwise, stillness prevailed. Twelve days after peace came, Phnom Penh and the other cities of Cambodia were peaceful at last.

On the highways, roads and trails of Cambodia, the 3,500,000 people—half the nation's population— wandered toward the jungles and a future they could not comprehend. In a way, they had been changed as much as the cities they departed. For they had been transformed into a spiritually paralyzed and physically trembling mass of prisoners who understood only that if they did not go on, they swiftly would be "reeducated" by their new master, *Angka Loeu*.

A young philosophy professor, Phal Oudam, was one of the legion that had greeted the soldiers of Angka Loeu as harbingers of peace. "Now, only seeing them walk, we, the population, are so much afraid. We tremble like half-drowned baby mice."

II

THE ORGANIZATION
ON HIGH

Angka Loeu in two stunning weeks began to realize an ageless revolutionary dream poetically expressed by Omar Khayyám nine centuries ago.

> Ah, Love! could thou and I with Fate conspire
> To grasp this sorry Scheme of Things entire
> Would not we shatter it to bits—and then
> Re-mould it nearer to the Heart's Desire!

The Organization on High was not interested in merely improving or even radically modifying existing Cambodian society. Rather, *Angka Loeu* was determined to "shatter it to bits" and start completely anew. For *Angka Loeu* had resolved to annul the past and obliterate the present so as to fashion a future uncontaminated by the influences of either.

Awed foreigners and benumbed Cambodians alike could not comprehend what they saw in Phnom Penh during the first days after the conquest. The emptying of the cities; the burning of books, markets and houses; the looting of stores and homes, not to acquire but to destroy valuables; the demolition of buildings; the desecration of temples; the smashing of automobiles, medical equipment and other products of foreign technology—all seemed like madness. Yet given the resolve of *Angka Loeu*, all it did was purposeful, consistent and logical.

By banishing life from the cities, *Angka Loeu* suddenly eradicated traditional patterns of life, detached the people from their past and largely reduced them to the same level, to one disoriented, malleable mass. On the highways leading from the cities, on the trails into the jungles, deeply rooted values and attitudes began to disintegrate. Owners of Mercedes and comparably costly automobiles desperately tried to trade cars for bicycles. Rice and makeshift pushcarts became more prized than gold and precious jewelry. Khmers who for centuries had honored the dead with extreme reverence robbed corpses of shoes and indifferently trampled over flattened bodies in the road. Status and distinction derived from attainment, position, rank, education, wealth or inheritance vanished. The second day of the exodus one of the richest merchants of Phnom Penh died on the highway a few kilometers from the city. A week before, thousands would have gathered at his funeral to offer homage. As it was, no one even paused while two relatives buried him in a shallow roadside grave marked by a bamboo pole.

Passing through outlying villages, exiles heard communist officers boast that *Angka Loeu* would build the only true communism, the only truly classless society in which everyone would be equal. Such boasts were not hollow. The millions cast from the cities were all at once equally homeless. They were or soon would be equally bereft of possessions, equally hungry, equally vulnerable to epidemics. In the countryside and jungles all would equally share the common labors and destiny *Angka Loeu* had decreed for them. All were and would remain equally at the mercy of *Angka Loeu*.

In assaulting the material manifestations of Cambodian culture and civilization, the communists were striking at the concepts the objects of their fury symbolized. And the assaults presaged systematic attempts to undermine or eliminate entirely the traditional concepts of family, home, religion, education, commerce and technology that formed the foundations of society.

Not surprisingly, therefore, of all targets of destruction, *Angka Loeu* assigned high priority to literature—books, periodicals, documents, records, manuscripts, correspondence, even identity cards. Literature articulated and preserved the concepts under siege. It enabled Cambodians to see and linked them with the rest of the world. It formed one of the strongest ties bonding together the past, present, and future of Cambodia. Hence, *Angka Loeu* set out to erase the printed and written word from the land and thereby to isolate Cambodians from their past, from the outside world and from one another.

Having emptied and vandalized the cities, *Angka Loeu* proclaimed the birth of "Democratic Cambodia" and proudly declared, "More than 2,000 years of Cambodian history have virtually ended." It is difficult to dispute that claim. Within a few days *Angka Loeu* had turned Cambodian society upside down.

Within a few days the "Organization on High" had advanced faster and further than any other revolutionaries of modern times toward the complete obliteration of an entire society.

The accomplishment was extraordinary by any standards. But its full magnitude can be appreciated only with an understanding of what the faceless mask and mysterious aura of *Angka Loeu* concealed—a handful of theorists who had started out with almost nothing except impregnable conviction that they knew what was best for everybody.

Probably fewer than two dozen persons controlled *Angka Loeu*, indeed were *Angka Loeu*. Dominant among them were:

Khieu Samphan, forty-four. Stoic and incorruptible, socially maladroit and shy, doctrinaire and dogmatic, Khieu had been educated as an economist but instead had consecrated himself to communism and revolution. The mild, inoffensive veneer of his personality masked an implacable will. And Khieu proved to be remorseless and pitiless in pursuit both of his ideals and his enemies.

Hou Yuon, forty-five. Intelligent and adventuresome, bold and sometimes arrogant, charismatic and a good leader, Hou had studied law and economics, become a teacher and then entered politics. Denounced as a subversive in 1967, he had escaped to the jungles, where he reputedly enjoyed combat and guerrilla life. Hou was very popular among his comrades and probably was the *Angka Loeu* leader most able to relate to ordinary Cambodians.

Hu Nim, forty-three. Although former associates portrayed Hu as nervous and rude, garrulous and even supercilious, he nevertheless commanded respect because of his intelligence and skill as a polemicist. Having been educated as a lawyer, Hu had held a number of governmental posts until 1967, when he had fled to the jungles after being exposed as a communist subversive. Alone among *Angka Loeu* chieftains, Hu liked to be known as a Don Juan, but his reputation as such may be founded mainly on his own boasting.

Son Sen, forty-five. Humorless and pedantic, hard and fanatical, Son had been a professor suspended from the National Pedagogical Institute in 1962 on grounds that he was subverting students. A few months later the government had accused him of fomenting student disturbances in Phnom Penh and Siem Reap. Anticipating arrest, Son had gone into hiding in 1963 and eventually had become a principal military leader of *Angka Loeu*.

Ieng Sary, forty-five. Shrewd and resolute, courteous and diplomatic, adept at intrigue and organization, Ieng had been a teacher who sought to convert students and intellectuals to communism. He had maintained contact with the Soviet and Chinese embassies in Phnom Penh until 1963, when he had disappeared to become a guerrilla leader. In terms of fervor and ruthlessness, few in *Angka Loeu* surpassed him.

Ieng Thirith, forty-three or forty-four. The beautiful wife of Ieng Sary had followed her husband underground in 1964 and had thereafter shared the rigors of insurgency with him. Apparently, she concentrated on recruitment and indoctrination of young people. She is regarded as even more of a zealot than her husband.

Saloth Sar, forty-seven. Quiet and retiring, patient

and determined, characterized by an opponent as dull and effeminate, Saloth had been a teacher and journalist. But he had devoted himself primarily to promotion of communism and by the late 1950s had been perhaps the most energetic party organizer in Cambodia. He had disappeared in 1963 and may have undergone training in North Vietnam before rejoining insurgents in the jungle.

Koy Thuon, forty-four or forty-five. Comparatively little is known about Koy except that he had been a teacher and key communist functionary who had dropped from sight in the early 1960s. He probably had been trained in North Vietnam and possibly also in China prior to returning to Cambodia as a guerrilla in 1968 or 1969.

These eight people who now exercised powers of life and death over 7,000,000 people were remarkably similar in background. All were from middle-class families; all had studied in France during the 1950s. In France all had joined the communist-infiltrated Union of Cambodian Students, and all had ardently embraced communism. Subsequently, all save Ieng Thirith had become members of the Central Committee of the clandestine Cambodian Communist Party. In the context of their values and beliefs, apparently all, except possibly Hu Nim, were principled, honest and brave and almost puritanical.

All had been educated as economists, lawyers or teachers. Although they were to glorify manual labor as the highest of endeavors, none had ever earned a living with his or her hands. None had ever managed any enterprise or undertaken any activity wherein performance was tested by objective measurement. All had spent roughly half their adult lives abroad or in the jungles isolated from the daily realities of their country. Yet all were certain that they had evolved theories that would give birth to an ideal country, and all were united in a fanatical determination to put their theories into practice, purely and absolutely, whatever the cost.

One of the dominant masters and leading theorists of *Angka Loeu* was Khieu Samphan, presently chief of state in Democratic Cambodia. Possibly his life and personality explain some of the *Angka Loeu* policies and deeds that seem most inexplicable. Khieu was born on July 27, 1931, the son of a judge who died allegedly after having been imprisoned or disgraced as a consequence of bribery. Khieu's mother, a thin wisp of a woman who was half Chinese, had reared him in Kompong Cham, earning a comfortable living by selling fruit and vegetables. A frail child beset by some respiratory ailment that caused his nose to run perpetually, Khieu was often seriously ill. A classmate who attended school with him both in Cambodia and France remembers:

"Khieu was a mediocre, quiet student whose most remarkable characteristics were passivity and total lack of aggressiveness. Maybe because of this, he attracted persecution. He was victimized by the whole class. We'd kick him, hit him, push him around, and he'd never once fight for himself. He had no defense, not even a verbal one. Anyone else would at least have shouted at his aggressor, insulted him. Not Khieu Samphan. All he used to cry was, 'Stop! Stop!' Maybe we children were treating him like this to make him come out of his passivity, to get at least a reaction. Even shouts of 'Stop! Stop!' were better than his unsmiling silence."

Cambodians always have regarded sex as a lovely integral of life, and upon attaining puberty, the boys in Khieu's class happily embarked upon the uninhibited courtship of girls. Khieu, though, soon dropped out of the chase because he had found himself impotent. With this discovery, he retreated into further isolation and loneliness.

Given a scholarship by the Cambodian government, Khieu arrived in Paris in 1954 and took a room at the Indochina House on the campus of City University. He may have sought medical advice regarding his impotence, for he told others the condition was permanent and incurable. As if to compensate for the void in his life, Khieu flung himself furiously first into his books, then into communism. His classmate recalls:

"In Paris we were immediately integrated into a group of Cambodian students already living there. Most were communists. The leader of the group was Thiounn Mom, an extremely brilliant boy and one of only two Khmers who ever managed to get into France's elite Polytechnical School. He was the head of the communist committee, and his prestige among all students from Southeast Asia was enormous. Three or four of them were studying architecture or engineering, and their math was not quite up to French standards. Thiounn Mom gave them free math lessons once a week. He was very devoted and took great interest in their academic progress. It is true that his math lessons were larded with communist propaganda and that he indoctrinated all of them.

"Khieu had boundless admiration for Thiounn Mom, and he became a communist under Thiounn Mom's tutoring. Yet Khieu was totally anonymous, harmless and in no way prominent. His isolation increased. Many times I'd go to his room, trying to convince him to go out on the town with me. He always refused.

"'I'm not interested in having a good time,' he'd say. 'I'm only interested in studying.'

"He indeed was immersed in his books all the time. In his room he must have had the complete collection of all the writings of Marx, Lenin and Engels."

Upon earning his doctorate in economics in 1959, Khieu returned to Cambodia and more torment. He lived in a hovel as a bachelor ascetic and traveled about Phnom Penh on a bicycle. Though penniless, he obtained from unknown sources enough money to found a small biweekly newspaper that published communist propaganda. In retaliation, the royalist police under Prince Sihanouk harassed him continuously. One morning thugs probably in the employ of the police cornered him on the street and beat him. Then they subjected him to an even more humiliating indignity by stripping off his clothes and marching him away naked. After allowing him to publish for about eighteen months, the government arbitrarily shut down his newspaper. As he had done when a boy, Khieu outwardly submitted to the persecution without protest.

The career and even the life of Khieu perhaps would have ended unnoticed in prison except for the political machinations of Prince Norodom Sihanouk. The erratic prince personally distrusted communists and hoped to steer Cambodia on a course toward democratic capitalism while preserving its independence through neutralism that played off East against

West.* "The policy to be followed is to accept that the influence of the communist bloc shall counterbalance the influence of the Western bloc. Henceforth we shall hold out one hand to the West and the other to the communists."

By the early 1960s, though, Sihanouk concluded that the communists were destined to triumph in Indochina and that Cambodian interests lay in currying their favor. He consequently adopted an appeasement policy that in time led him to establish ties with Hanoi and the Vietcong and mount propaganda campaigns against South Vietnam and break relations with Saigon and Washington. At the same time he sought to offset the influence of rightists within Cambodia by according leftists a measure of power. Thus, in 1962 Prince Sihanouk allowed Khieu Samphan to run for the National Assembly as a member of his own political front and thereby assured him election. Additionally, he gave Khieu the cabinet post of secretary of state for commerce.

However, the antigovernment agitation of the communists and other radicals so incensed the prince that in 1963 he publicly branded several of them subversives. Believing that the excoriation presaged their arrest, some of the radicals, including Ieng Sary and Son Sen, decamped for the jungles, North Vietnam or China. Under pressure, Khieu Samphan resigned from his cabinet position, yet retained his seat in the National Assembly.

Perhaps because Khieu seemed meek and indis-

*Once he publicly referred to Cambodian communists as "traitorous bloodsuckers."

posed toward violence, perhaps because his radical
orations were delivered so tediously that they bored
rather than incited, Khieu was not repressed during
the next four years. Plodding but unwavering, he
continued to speak out against the government
openly and conspire against it covertly. Then in 1967
riots broke out in Battambang Province, and correctly
or not, Prince Sihanouk blamed the communists. In
another fit of exasperation, he singled out Khieu
Samphan, Hu Nim and Hou Yuon as traitors. Fearing
for their lives, the three ran to join insurgents in the
jungles. They vanished so completely and kept their
subsequent whereabouts so concealed that baseless
and romanticized stories about them flourished.
Someone, perhaps the prince himself, dubbed them
the Three Phantoms, and the term adhered, endowing
them with a certain charisma and mystique in the
mind of the general public. But among those who had
known Khieu in Phnom Penh, he enjoyed neither
charisma nor mystique. They still thought of him as
an innocuous, timid bachelor, honest and idealistic,
yet dogmatic and hopelessly impractical.

If it seemed improbable that Khieu Samphan ever
would perform great feats of any kind, it seemed even
more improbable that the insurgents he was to lead
ever could prevail in Cambodia. They numbered
probably no more than 2,000 men, a motley, disunited
assortment of communist intellectuals from the cities,
disaffected ethnic minorities and jungle bandits. The
few hundred communists were disorganized, poorly
armed with old bolt-action French rifles and widely
rejected as agents of an alien ideology hostile to
Khmer traditions and religion. Among the Cambodian peasantry the classic requisites of revolution

simply did not exist, a fact evidenced by communist failure over two decades to arouse any real support in the countryside whatsoever. As a minute band of outcasts unable to expand through force of arms or ideas, the insurgents were little more than a nuisance. They might well have languished indefinitely and ineffectually in the jungles had not a series of fortunate events intervened in their behalf.

For a while the diplomatic maneuvers and intrigues of Prince Sihanouk succeeded. Secretly he collaborated with the North Vietnamese and Vietcong, permitting them to ship large quantities of supplies through the port of Sihanoukville across Cambodia into South Vietnam. Even more helpfully, he tacitly approved large-scale violations of Cambodian territory by the North Vietnamese, allowing them to establish sanctuaries and supply routes adjacent to South Vietnam. By 1969 elements of five North Vietnamese divisions, comprising between 40,000 and 50,000 troops, maintained operational bases on Cambodian soil. In return, the North Vietnamese carefully limited aid to the Cambodian insurgents and otherwise tried to avoid antagonizing the prince.

The diplomatic acrobatics of Sihanouk, together with his flamboyant personality, gained him certain prestige on the world scene. Some journalists even likened him to his great ancestors, the "god-kings," whose Machiavellian ploys had sustained Cambodia through its age of grandeur. But collusion with the Vietnamese, against whom Cambodians harbor an ancient, almost venomous animosity, caused problems at home. The armed occupation of Cambodian territory and the highly visible presence of Vietnamese manning the supply line through

Sihanoukville provoked increasing protests and hostility in Phnom Penh. Sihanouk himself appears to
have been angered by the widening encroachment of
the North Vietnamese and by sporadic, probably unplanned skirmishes between the communists and his
own forces. In any case, in 1969 he ordered Prime
Minister Lieutenant General Lon Nol to organize "a
government of national salvation" ostensibly to defend the country.

On March 8, 1970, while Prince Sihanouk was in
France, peasants in Svay Rieng Province demonstrated against the presence of North Vietnamese
troops on Cambodian soil. Three days later a massive
demonstration in support of the peasants occurred in
Phnom Penh. Thousands of students, soldiers and
monks rampaged through the streets of the capital
and sacked the North Vietnamese and Vietcong embassies. In Paris, Prince Sihanouk accused rightists of
plotting to embarrass him. He indignantly flew off to
Moscow and refused to receive a delegation dispatched by Lon Nol to explain the demonstrations.
On March 18 the National Assembly voted unani-
mously to remove Prince Sihanouk as chief of state
and vest full power in Lon Nol, who already was
prime minister.

Because Sihanouk remained, among the peasantry,
a popular symbol of the "god- king" tradition deeply
embedded in Khmer culture, Lon Nol invited him to
come home as a nonpolitical constitutional monarch.
Instead, the prince flew from Moscow to Peking, took
up residence there under the patronage of his good
friend Chou En-lai and ceremoniously tore to pieces
the conciliatory cable from Lon Nol. The next day
North Vietnamese Premier Pham Van Dong landed in
Peking and offered the prince "a couple of thousand

of the best [military instructors] we have." On March 23, five days after his ouster, Prince Sihanouk joined the communists in a coalition, the National United Front of Cambodia, to fight the Lon Nol government. Shortly afterward the coalition formed an exile government in Peking, the Royal Government of National Union, with Sihanouk as its titular head. And from a jungle redoubt in Cambodia, Khieu Samphan, Hu Nim and Hou Yuon, in their first public act since 1967, sent a message to the prince whose scorn had forced them to run for their lives: "If you, the traditional leader of the Cambodian people, decide to fight with us—we demand nothing better."

Thus, through little enterprise of their own, the Cambodian communists almost overnight achieved a textbook objective of communists everywhere—a coalition that cloaked them with respectability and put at their disposal the resources of others. Stigmatized as foreign agents, they could not attract popular support. Now, with their real identity and aims obscured in the coalition, they would appeal to the people in the name of a prince trusted and esteemed by much of the populace. As proof that they were legitimate nationalists, they had only to point to the royal embrace of the prince.

On March 29, just six days after formation of the coalition, North Vietnamese troops sprang from their sanctuaries and in the name of the prince attacked Lon Nol forces and began occupying as much of the western and northwestern provinces of Cambodia as they could. They studiously avoided appealing to the people as communists. Rather, they represented that they simply were attempting to restore Sihanouk to his rightful throne.

A month later, on April 30, with the North

Vietnamese engaged against a new enemy, American and South Vietnamese divisions invaded Cambodia in a massive surprise attack on the communist sanctuaries. The involvement of American ground forces in this "limited incursion," as Washington characterized it, lasted only sixty days and succeeded militarily. It inflicted severe personnel and material losses on the communists, forced them to abate battlefield pressures in South Vietnam and thereby reduced casualties suffered by the Americans withdrawing from Vietnam.

However, the invasion, accompanied by devastating B-52 raids, served to push the retreating North Vietnamese and Vietcong even farther into Cambodia. When the Americans pulled out, they left the communists in effective control of larger areas of the country than ever before. The insurgents led by Khieu Samphan moved into these areas protected by Vietnamese communists who had initially done virtually all the fighting. They were reinforced by the arrival of Cambodian communists, perhaps as many as 6,000, whom Hanoi over the years had secretly recruited, trained and kept in reserve in North Vietnam. Through outside intervention, luck and their own dogged persistence, the men who were to compose Angka Loeu now for the first time had territory and significant strength with which to work.

They also had new opportunities. To escape the spreading fighting, people started swarming from the countryside into the cities, spawning economic and social problems for the Lon Nol government. The American intervention and B-52 raids (the latter continued until August 1973) enabled the communists somewhat more convincingly to depict the North Vietnamese as "our teachers," the United States as the "imperialist aggressor" and the Lon Nol government as "a lackey of the imperialists." The *Far Eastern Economic Review* observed: "From being widely regarded as the dogmatic disciples of a Marxist ideology alien to Khmer national traditions and culture, the Khmer Rouge became patriots."

With formation of the coalition, the immediate aim of the Cambodian communists became not to marshal military strength for an assault on the presumed common enemy in Phnom Penh, but to secure undivided, if hidden, control of the coalition. Perhaps remembering the lessons learned from communist textbooks in Paris, Khieu Samphan and his colleagues swiftly maneuvered toward this end. At the birth of the coalition government the Three Phantoms arranged key posts for themselves. Khieu Samphan was deputy prime minister and national defense minister; Hu Nim, minister of information and propaganda; and Hou Yuon, minister of the interior, communal reforms and cooperatives. In September 1970 the National United Front Radio announced appointment of ten "vice-ministers" of the coalition government, all of whom were in the jungles of Cambodia. The Three Phantoms headed the list, which also included Ieng Thirith. On paper and generally in the eyes of the world, control of the Royal Government of National Union still rested with Prince Sihanouk and his royalist ministers in Peking. In reality, it had shifted to Khieu Samphan and his fellow fugitives in Cambodia. Prince Sihanouk himself candidly acknowledged this reality during a significant but little-noticed interview, granted Agence France-Presse in Peking on September 26, 1970. The news agency reported: "Prince Norodom Sihanouk said today that the majority of the Royal Government of

National Union is now Red Khmer, and the power already belongs to the Cambodian Communist Party. 'I am giving everything to the Red Khmers.'"

However, dominance of the upper levels of the co-alition and insurgency movement was far from enough for the communists. They were determined to extend their grip down through every echelon of the insurgency forces and to ensure that they, not any adherents of the prince, ruled all people and territory falling into their domain. While accepting recruits lured to them by the magnetism of the prince, they methodically purged followers who persisted in evincing loyalty to him. At the same time they made certain that the cadre trained in North Vietnam and suspected of being beholden to Hanoi did not attain positions of influence.

Prince Sihanouk realized what was happening. In another burst of candor, he told journalist Oriana Fallaci during an interview in June 1973: "The Khmer Rouge do not like me at all, and I know that. Ooh la la! I understand quite well that they only tolerate me because without me they cannot prevail over the peasants, and without the peasant, one can make no revolution in Cambodia. It is clear to me. When they no longer need me, they will spit me out like a cherry pit."

Nevertheless, the prince still lent his name to the insurgency and, in the words of Roger Kershaw of the University of Kent in England, "incessantly pro-claimed the moderate, nationalist, essentially pro-gressive and not in any sense communist character of the Khmer Rouge." By continuing to serve as a front, Sihanouk helped perpetuate a widely accepted myth that persisted even after the fall of Phnom Penh. Ac-cording to it, the leadership of the insurgency was divided among three distinct, disparate factions: the in-country communists or Khmer Rouge, led by the Three Phantoms and other French-educated Marxists; the Hanoi-oriented communists, who had trained and hibernated in North Vietnam, and the more moderate, nationalistic followers of Prince Sihanouk. From this myth of shared leadership flowed the delusion that counterbalancing influences from the three factions would result in compromises and produce a government which would be reasonable, even if communist.

The communists did all they could to preserve this useful myth and to maintain the façade of a coalition adorned by royalty. In propaganda directed at Cambodians in unconquered territory and at the rest of the world, they continuously invoked the aura of the prince and extolled him as leader of the war against the corrupt Lon Nol. And they acquiesced to a formal proclamation of coalition aims that sounded eminently reasonable. The declaration, issued in Paris, solemnly pledged that the coalition would welcome "with understanding" the "popular masses, functionaries, policemen, officers, noncommissioned officers and simple soldiers in the army of the Lon Nol-Sirik Matak* clique, intellectuals, students and notables," even "those who, for a variety of reasons, cannot yet join [the coalition]." In conciliatory and politically liberal terms, the announced program guaranteed, except to "known traitors," the "freedom to vote, the freedom to stand for election, the freedom of speech, of the press, of opinion, of association; the

---

*Sisowath Sirik Matak was a leading figure in the Lon Nol government. He was executed by the communists after the fall of Phnom Penh.

freedom to demonstrate, to reside in or travel throughout the country, to travel abroad." It promised "to protect the inviolability of individuals, of property, of goods and of the correspondence of all Cambodians . . . to protect and guarantee rights for lands and property, according to national law."

However, in sections of Cambodia the communists had overrun, they ceased mentioning Sihanouk, except to disparage him. And they so thoroughly purged his adherents from the upper echelons of the insurgency that when the prince and his entourage returned in September 1975, they could find not one of the old friends left behind in 1970. Significantly, though, prior to their victory, communist leaders even in areas securely within their domain preferred not to call popular attention to the fact that they were communists, and they rarely referred to themselves as such. Instead, they began to call themselves *Angka Loeu.*

By early 1973 Prince Sihanouk, as he himself sensed and in so many words confessed, was no more than a figurehead. The North Vietnamese had withdrawn their divisions, diverting most to South Vietnam. Khieu Samphan and the tiny coterie of French-educated communists had gathered into their hands complete control of the insurgency forces, which they had multiplied to at least 35,000 troops by recruiting in the magic name of Sihanouk and by mass enforced conscription in the occupied villages. Now they were ready to begin the final military assault that would deliver all Cambodia into their hands.

In retrospect, it is evident that by late 1973 Khieu Samphan and colleagues had also completed the grand design of the new Cambodia they proposed to construct upon destruction of the old. Outlines of this society were discernible as early as 1972. Captured communist soldiers began telling government soldiers what they obviously had heard from their superiors—that, once victorious, *Angka Loeu* intended to run everybody out of the cities. And in occupied areas of Kampot, Takeo and Kandal provinces the communists actually did uproot whole villages and scatter the inhabitants into the jungles. They also instituted well-planned programs of collectivization, ideological indoctrination, torture and terror, all accompanied by massive onslaught against fundamental Khmer traditions and institutions. Kenneth M. Quinn, a State Department specialist on Cambodia, in early 1974 made a scholarly analysis of communist actions in the occupied territories and found clear precedents for most of their actions after April 17, 1975.* Quinn perceived that the communists had committed themselves to "total social revolution" and had determined that all belonging to the past "was anathema and must be destroyed." He concluded that to accomplish total revolution, the communists were attempting "to psychologically reconstruct individual members of society." In his extensively researched analysis, he wrote:

    ... This process entails stripping away, through terror and other means, the traditional bases, structures and forces which have shaped and guided an

*Quinn submitted his findings to the State Department on February 20, 1974. An excised version of his report was declassified by the Department. The essence of his original report also appears in a treatise, *Political Change in Wartime; The Khmer Krahom Revolution in Southern Cambodia 1970–1974*, delivered to the American Political Science Association Convention on September 4, 1975, in San Francisco.

individual's life until he is left as an atomized, isolated individual unit; and then rebuilding him according to party doctrine by substituting a series of
new values, organizations and ethical norms for the
ones taken away. The first half of this process can be
found in the KK [communist] attack on religion, the
destruction of vestiges of the Sihanouk regime, attacks on parental and monastical authority, prohibi-
tions on traditional songs and dances, and the use of
terror. Psychological atomization, which can result
from these practices and which causes individuals to
feel effectively isolated from the rest of their community, can be seen to have actually occurred. Refugees
from Kampot and Kandal provinces have said they
were so afraid of arrest and execution that even in
their own homes they dared not utter a critical word
and obediently complied with every KK [communist]
directive.

The process Quinn describes, of course, was not an
original invention of *Angka Loeu*. Variants of it can be
found in Aristotle's analyses of tyranny, in communist literature, in the history of the Soviet Union
and other totalitarian states. But it is difficult to find a
precise precedent for the totality and barbarity with
which *Angka Loeu* was prepared to apply the process,
against men, women and children alike.

Probably there was no one architect of the new
society *Angka Loeu* conceived for Cambodia or any
single designer of the methods by which it planned to
build the society. Considering the similarity of background and outlook of the *Angka Loeu* leadership, it
seems more likely that the fundamental program
adopted was a collective creation. However, the ori-
gins of some of the more extreme policies may lie in
the personality of the impotent ideologue Khieu

Samphan. Transient impotence can be the result of many mundane causes, but numerous psychiatrists consider that chronic impotence, unless inflicted by physical factors, is the product of profound hostility. Certainly, Khieu Samphan, the sickly, bullied child, the friendless, tormented youth, the meek, persecuted man, had reason to be hostile. Perhaps some of the deathly hostility *Angka Loeu* was to visit upon the Cambodian people, such as the savage slaughter of women and children as well as men, the ferocious assault on the Khmer traditions of love, courtship and family, the draconian punishment of extramarital sex, was spawned by the hostility of the unloved and unloving Khieu.

That obviously is a matter of conjecture. But what is in doubt is not so important as what is certain. Khieu Samphan and a few kindred people, who neither by achievements nor by ideas had ever attracted any substantial following, absconded into the jungles, assumed leadership of an insignificant, ineffectual little guerrilla force, captured control of a political coalition and through it absolute control of an entire society.

Attaining absolute control, they converted all Cambodia into a social laboratory and all Cambodians into experimental specimens. In their laboratory they were free to implement their theories unrestrained by external influences, unhampered by the past, uninhibited by practical experience. Having shattered Cambodian society to bits, they now were free to "Re-mould it nearer to the Heart's Desire!"

III

PURIFICATION OF
THE POPULATION

Sem Vann was a tough, handsome, intelligent sergeant major who did not welcome peace at any price. The twenty-seven-year-old son of peasants, Sem for nearly eight years had fought first the Vietnamese, then the Cambodian communists, and he was prepared to fight them indefinitely. His infantry unit, flown in to reinforce the defenses of Battambang airport, had acquitted itself bravely in some of the fiercest combat of the war. But on April 17 the communists completely encircled the airfield, and not long afterward the defenders heard the forlorn government broadcast from the capital, 250 kilometers to the southeast. "Phnom Penh is in the hands of the Khmer Rouge," said the voice of General Mey Sichan. "I am asking all soldiers of the governmental army, wherever they are, to lay down their arms."

Sem felt the command was a mistake. Having seen what the communists had done in war, he feared what they would do in peace. Moreover, his heavily armed men were, like himself, both able and willing to resist further, from the jungle if need be. Yet as a mere sergeant he had no choice except to obey, and upon seeing 100 or so of the enemy approaching in their familiar black dress, he put down his M-16 rifle.

Silently, Sem followed the dictates of the victors. They directed the government troops back to their barracks, allowed them to pack their belongings and marched them to the lycée (high school) in Battambang. At the school the communists distributed rice and authorized their captives to buy whatever else they wanted at a nearby marketplace which still offered an abundance of food. Aside from convening a brief assembly to boast of their triumph, the communists that first day left the prisoners alone.

Among the defeated troops a mood of relief, even euphoria, grew with realization that they were being treated fairly and that no longer would Cambodians have to kill Cambodians. If many shared Sem's apprehensions, their anxiety was not apparent. Although the communists were not friendly, they were acting reasonably. Their behavior seemed to bear out the widely quoted pledge made by Prince Sihanouk on March 20. "There will not be any bloodbath if the armed units of the Phnom Penh regime lay down their arms. These people will be reprieved."

Thus, even though the hundreds of government personnel congregating at the school soon far outnumbered the fifty or so guards posted there, it did not occur to them to try to escape or overpower their wardens. As instructed, they discarded their uniforms and changed to civilian clothes. Sem and most of his unit also tore up their military identification papers and threw them away. As more and more soldiers surrendered themselves and their weapons, huge stacks of rifles, grenade launchers, machine guns and ammunition piled up at barracks and police stations around the city.

The next day, Friday, Battambang radio repeatedly ordered all military men to report to the Groupe Centre primary school. By late afternoon more than 1,000 officers, 2,000 noncoms and 1,000 soldiers—the bulk of the government forces in the area—were milling about the school and its grounds. Politely, the communists told them to segregate by rank. Commissioned officers were to move to the So Hoe primary school next door, enlisted personnel were to join the others at the lycée and noncoms were to stay at the Groupe Centre.

But while these instructions were being issued, a rapidly spreading rumor caused such consternation among the prisoners that the communists took notice. The report concerned Colonel Tan Pok, a physician and chief of Military Hospital 403. Colonel Tan was a short, rotund, gentle doctor in his forties who had a pretty young wife and several children. He was well known and esteemed in Battambang because of his willingness to treat anyone, civilian or military, who needed help, whatever the hour.

According to the rumor, the Khmer Rouge had degraded Colonel Tan by making him walk some 8 kilometers along the highway toward Pailin and into the jungle near Prey Kone Khla. There they shot him and a dozen or more members of his medical staff.

The communists, perhaps fearing disorder among their captives, who still greatly outnumbered them, chose to confirm the execution and try to justify it.

Guards declared that Colonel Tan had been "a bad civil servant . . . a valet of the imperialists . . . a Lon Nol puppet . . . an enemy of the people." Moreover, he was a bad doctor. He deserved to die.

To those who knew Colonel Tan, the explanations were so at variance with reality that in a way they shocked as much as did the execution. As the euphoria of peace ebbed, Sergeant Major Sem glimpsed the darkness ahead and acted accordingly. Instead of joining his fellow noncommissioned officers at the Groupe Centre, he demoted himself and remained with the privates at the lycée.

The next morning a communist announcement dramatically restored the morale of the government forces. Prince Sihanouk was returning to Cambodia! Soon he would fly from exile in Peking to Phnom Penh for victory celebrations. To welcome the prince, officers at the So Hoe school would travel to the capital for the celebration. In keeping with the moment of the occasion, all officers were to put on dress uniforms with full decorations preparatory to the journey.

Although the officers had fought for the Khmer Republic which had replaced Sihanouk's monarchy, a residue of goodwill toward the prince remained. All the officers and men had grown up in a Cambodia dominated by the prince's extraordinary personality and leadership. Most had seen him in his endless tours of the country; many had met him personally. Perhaps the old tranquil times would return with the prince. After all, now that the war was over and his side had won, was he not once again *Samdech Euv*, the "Prince Father"? Not only was he returning, instilling the voice of paternal moderation to the upper

councils of the Khmer Rouge, but he magnanimously
had also decided to honor the defeated army, to bring
it into the new nation's embrace by permitting its
officers to take part in welcoming celebrations.

At the So Hoe school, joy was barely restrained. A
young lieutenant boasted to Sergeant Major Thach
Ngy about his good fortune. "You're not an officer, so
of course you cannot come," he said, somewhat con-
descendingly. "You'll be working in the rice paddies.
But be patient and accept your fate." Thach, a hardened twenty-six-year-old military policeman, was
not envious—he had already resolved to escape to
Thailand, and Battambang was much closer to the
border than Phnom Penh. Moreover, there was something odd, he thought, about the announced ar-
rangements for the officers' trip. "It isn't settled yet on
what date we'll meet the prince," the lieutenant had
told him, "so we have to take food for three days with
us." Why would the officers chosen to meet the prince
have to take their own food? And a three-day trip?
That was about how long it would take to march to
Phnom Penh if the officers went almost nonstop. But
why would these chosen few be made to walk?

At about 11 A.M. trucks drove up to the school.
Some 315 of the 1,000 officers, including the young
lieutenant, were selected for these first vehicles.
Afraid that they might eventually be left behind,
many of the men who had not been picked ran after
the vehicles, trying to jump on as the trucks pulled
away. Several succeeded, helped by comrades already aboard.

Kom Kiry, a fifty-two-year-old infantry major, was
one of the officers who departed for Phnom Penh that
morning. There were nine vehicles in the convoy: in

the lead, a jeep and a Land-Rover holding a total of about twenty armed communists; then a bus with some thirty officers and ten guards; five open trucks carrying only government officers; and, bringing up the rear, a sixth truck containing about sixty communists.

In Kom's truck there was a festive air. A communist official named Khek Pen had passed the word that after the welcoming ceremonies in Phnom Penh, all the officers would be given a certificate absolving them of any blame for serving in Lon Nol's army. They then would be free to return to their families.

For some three hours the convoy drove along Highway 5 toward Phnom Penh. Abruptly, at about 2:30 P.M. near Kbal Damrei village not far from Mount Tippadei, the lead jeep turned off the main bitumen onto a secondary road leading toward the Battambang–Phnom Penh railroad tracks. As the rest of the convoy also turned sharply right, the officers, who had been joking and laughing, suddenly hushed. They could see, waiting on the right side of the road approximately 500 meters from the main highway, a line of perhaps sixty armed communist soldiers.

"We're stopping to eat?" someone asked hopefully.

"No," said Phim Uon, a forty-two-year-old major sitting near Kom, "we are going to be eaten."

The bus and trucks halted in a line beside the waiting soldiers, the vehicles about 50 meters apart. The officers were ordered to disembark. The convoy then pulled away, carrying with it the luggage the passengers had packed for Phnom Penh. Meantime, the rear truck had pulled up near the highway turnoff. The truckload of communists jumped off and deployed themselves.

Realizing now what awaited them, many officers began praying. However, Kom and Phim, who were still next to each other, studied the terrain. On the right-hand side of the road coming from the highway were soldiers; on the other were a field and, in the distance, a forest.

Perhaps ten minutes after the vehicles had driven off, a burst of machine-gun fire—about twenty rounds —came from the highway. A signal, thought Kom. About a minute later soldiers along the road began shooting into the officers. At the first sound of gunfire Phim and Kom slipped away from their group in a low crouch, then broke into a desperate run, heading for the forest.

An explosion nearby jarred them, and bullets hissed all about them. Phim was hit in the face and inside the left thigh; Kom in the upper right arm. Flesh wounds—so they kept on running. As Kom reached the edge of the forest, he saw Phim and two other majors crashing into the line of trees ahead of him.

For three hours the Khmer Rouge fired into the piles of dead and dying officers. Hiding in the dense undergrowth, Kom could hear the distinctive sounds of Khmer Rouge weaponry: AK-47 machine guns; B-40 rockets; M-81 mortars; 75 mm Chinese fieldpieces. Above the field of slaughter rose a thick pall of dust and smoke and the cries of the mangled and dying. Of the 315 officers in that convoy, only four—Kom, Phim and the majors spotted by Kom— appear to have escaped.

At the lycée Sergeant Major Sem and the 1,000 or so soldiers among whom he mingled heard nothing of the departed officers. They hoped for news of the welcoming celebrations in Phnom Penh, but there was none. Five days after the officers left, the communists evicted the civilian population from Battambang, and three days later they released the enlisted personnel at the high school, telling them they should make their way back to their native villages.

Hoping to return to his home in Takeo and find his parents, whom he had not seen in eight years, Sem boarded a train said to be leaving Battambang for Phnom Penh. Aboard he encountered many wives and children planning to rejoin the officers who had gone to greet Prince Sihanouk. The train progressed southward only about 40 kilometers before halting on a broad plain near Mount Tippadei where recent fighting had wrecked a section of the track. Railroad workers descended and began repair work. With about thirty-five Khmer Rouge guarding them, the passengers, most of them soldiers or relatives of military men, disembarked and made camp under nearby trees.

Sem and some friends walked ahead of the train a couple of kilometers to the Mount Tippadei railway station, where they slept for two nights. On the third day of their stay the party of young men fell into conversation with three female Khmer Rouge soldiers—black-clad country girls no older then seventeen, armed as heavily as their male colleagues and totally unsmiling. When Sem told one of them that he planned to rejoin his family in Takeo, the girl replied, "You had better leave early tomorrow morning then. And *don't* leave with the officers' families."

After discussing this strange and vaguely ominous remark, Sem and fourteen other soldiers decided not to wait for the train but to follow the girl's advice and go south on foot. Very early the next morning they began walking along the railroad track in the direction of Phnom Penh.

They had gone hardly 100 meters when they spotted the first bodies. They were sprawled all over a field near the railroad tracks. All were attired in dress uniforms, for they were the Battambang officers chosen to welcome Sihanouk.

Despite the horrors he had experienced in combat, nothing affected Sem as much as this massacre scene. "There were hundreds of them. The fifteen of us on the tracks were revolted. All our commanding officers were lying there dead. I realized I had been right when I didn't want to surrender."

The overpowering stench of unburied bodies rotting in the sun blighted a large area around Mount Tippadei for many weeks. Because so many people trekking northwestward toward their old villages or the Thai border followed the railroad tracks, countless Cambodians saw the corpses and told others of the macabre sight. The Mount Tippadei massacre thus became notorious in Cambodia, if not in the rest of the world.

It was only one of many organized massacres perpetrated throughout Cambodia during the first days after the surrender, and some of the lesser-known atrocities were even more barbaric. Despite their pledges of forgiveness and reconciliation, the communists immediately set out to exterminate the government officer corps and management echelon of the civil service. The massacres were committed on such a large scale and with such a basic sameness of method as to remove any doubt that *Angka Loeu* had planned them well before the war ended. Frequently the communists made little or no effort to conceal the atrocities, leaving unburied or only partially buried bodies in locales where they were certain to be seen.

The day after the Mount Tippadei massacre, April 20, the communists repeated in the town of Mongkol Borei the artifice they employed in Battambang. They marshaled government troops at a middle school in the town and a high school at Svay, about 3 kilometers away. Having hauled away surrendered weapons, they announced that officers would journey to Phnom Penh to hail Prince Sihanouk. Jubilant scenes similar to those in Battambang occurred at the middle school as more than 200 officers in dress uniforms clambered aboard trucks which drove away at midday.

About 8 kilometers south of Mongkol Borei on Highway 5 near the Japanese Agricultural Research Center, Me Chbar, the trucks halted. The mystified officers were ordered into a field beside the road. Suddenly tremendous explosions erupted all about them. The communists had heavily seeded the area beforehand with Claymore mines, which they detonated as the prisoners reached the center of the minefield.

As clouds of dirt and dust cleared, the communists threw hand grenades at clusters of screaming wounded. Still there were cries and slight movement from some of the mutilated and bloody bodies. A squad armed with pistols moved through the corpse-strewn field, administering coups de grâce. Pushed into three large heaps by bulldozers, the bodies were left to decompose in the tropical sun.

At Sisophon some 60 kilometers northwest of Battambang, government soldiers were mustered at a high school, the Lycée Sisophon. There was no mention here of Sihanouk's imminent arrival, but a Khmer Rouge with a loudspeaker told all officers that they should put on well-pressed uniforms and correct badges of rank. Once they were ready, they would be taken to Battambang and from there to Angkor, the capital of the ancient Cambodian Empire.

Soon three trucks arrived, picked up the officers—more than 200—and headed southeast out of Sisophon. But like their Battambang comrades, they did not travel very far. Near the village of O Taki the convoy halted, and the men were ordered to walk down a trail into the jungle. Less than a kilometer from the highway, machine guns concealed in the foliage opened up at close range from all sides. The ambush was so well prepared that although a few officers escaped into the underbrush, most were killed within minutes.

A few days later the communists evidently perpetrated another large massacre in the vicinity of the Research Center. In late April a forty-nine-year-old farmer, Dang Yim, saw hundreds of fresh bodies in fields by the Bek Treng crossroads on Highway 5, 26 kilometers northwest of Battambang. According to Dang, the killings here began about April 27. He understood that most of the victims came from Battambang, believing they were en route to welcome Prince Sihanouk. Though this understanding was based on hearsay, the farmer's account may explain the fate of officers who remained in Battambang after the Mount Tippadei massacre.

Elsewhere the communists invented similarly plausible but spurious stories to create a false tranquillity in their doomed prisoners. The seventeen officers in the government force defending Preah Net Preah, in Battambang Province, were told that they were being sent to Angkor Wat, some 90 kilometers to the east, for courses in "the new communist theory." Instead, they were taken to a spot about 3 kilometers west of the district office in nearby Chuk village and battered to death with clubs. The district chief at Chuk was killed along with them.

The same promises of safe passage to "reeducation" classes at Angkor Wat were made to sixty or so officers at the provincial capital of Samrong in Battambang's adjoining province of Oddar Meanchey. Here the communist issued the officers commandeered Honda motorcycles, one to every two officers. Led by only two Khmer Rouge soldiers, also on a Honda, the convoy set off on the highway south toward Angkor. Less than 30 kilometers from Samrong, however, the two Khmer Rouge made a short detour to Chong Kal village, and the officers unsuspectingly followed. As the group stopped and dismounted, the area seemed strangely empty of villagers—they had all been required to attend a meeting at a pagoda some distance to the east. In their place was a reception committee of about 100 Khmer Rouge soldiers, who overpowered the officers, tied their hands behind their backs and marched them about 6 kilometers to the point where the highway crosses the Stung Sen River. Here they clubbed all the prisoners to death and buried them in two mass graves.

Although eyewitness accounts are lacking, numerous refugees heard that large numbers of officers and civil servants continued to be executed during May at or around the Japanese Agricultural Research Center near Me Chbar. Chheng Savan, a twenty-nine-year-

old gem prospector exiled from Pailin, stopped at the
house of a friend in the village of Paoy Anchey near
the center in late May. While the family was eating an
evening meal, bursts of automatic rifle fire resounded, and Chheng's hosts looked terrified. An old
man said to him, "My friend, when you hear such rifle
fire, you can be sure it does not come from soldiers
who are hunting or amusing themselves. People are
being shot this very minute. Every day people are
being shot at the Japanese rice farm. I can take you
there and show you the bodies. Many officers have
been shot there. There are so many bodies at the
Japanese rice farm that looking at them makes you
dizzy."

All over Cambodia people saw the grisly evidence
of other massacres, although not the actual killing.
Approximately 120 bloated bodies of officers and civilians were observed on the shores of Lake Boeun
Thom near Koki in late April. More than 100 bodies of
officers, neatly lined up and decaying for all to see,
lay along the railroad track near the Svay Daunkeo
station on the border dividing Battambang and Pursat
provinces. The remains of approximately 300 officers, killed by machine-gun fire, were scattered over
rice fields outside the village of Veal Trea near
Mongkol Borei. The putrefying bodies of several
hundred—perhaps as many as 700—officers
slaughtered in fields outside the village of O Koki
west of Battambang emitted another massive stench.

As former government officers realized they all had
been condemned, it became more difficult to round
them up in large groups and dupe them into proceeding docilely to their death. Many of them adopted
new identities or otherwise attempted to hide their

military records. But *Angka* continued to hunt them down and kill them individually wherever they were unmasked. Most refugees interviewed by the authors reported having seen the lone corpses or clusters of two or three bodies of soldiers and officers along highways, outside villages, in the jungle or in rivers and lakes.

By failing to bury the slain, the communists advertised their deeds. It was as if *Angka Loeu* deliberately had chosen to turn the entire countryside into a ghastly corpse-strewn nightmare to intimidate the populace. Indeed, the communists frequently boasted of the killings. An officer told a group of exiles passing through Pursat that nineteen truckloads of military men had been taken from that city and liquidated. And in some villages *Angka* chieftains took people out of their way to see corpses.

In May eighty-eight Cambodians, including eighty-two air force pilots who had been training in Thailand before the fall of Phnom Penh, asked to be repatriated. For the benefit of Thai photographers at the border town of Poipet, the communists staged a gala welcoming ceremony. While Bangkok newspapers published photographs showing the repatriates receiving hearty handshakes, the communists transported them to the Svay Pagoda near Sisophon, relieved them of all their belongings and bound their hands behind their backs. Later they drove the eighty-two pilots in trucks to a field near the pagoda. The trucks had rear gates which could be narrowly opened so that only one person at a time could step down. As each pilot disembarked, soldiers bayoneted or clubbed him to death. In the trucks the pilots waiting their turn to die screamed in panic and hysteria. It took about two hours to kill them all. Afterward *Angka Loeu* through a domestic radio broadcast announced that the "traitors" had been executed.

Perhaps in the first massacres of officers, *Angka Loeu* was exacting revenge and at the same time attempting to crush the embryo of opposition. But it would seem that there was an additional motive. For the extermination of the officer corps was part of a broader program of calculated killing instituted immediately after the conquest. While "cleansing" the cities, *Angka Loeu* also undertook to "purify" the population by purging it of persons judged too physically or morally unfit to be redeemed.

A few days after the fall of Phnom Penh a communist soldier strode up to a blind beggar sleeping on the ground by the temple at Prek Phnov, about 9 kilometers north of the capital. Giving no warning, the soldier thrust his bayonet into the stomach of the beggar, killing him. As the black-clad executioner walked away, an onlooker, braver than most, asked him, "Why did you kill that man?"

The soldier answered, "He could never work in the fields. He was useless to society. It is better for him to die."

After the evacuation the communists for a while kept open one hospital in Phnom Penh, the Soviet Hospital. Kem Phaly, the medical student who evaded the evacuation order for a time by pretending to be a patient unable to move, ultimately earned the favor of the communists by treating their wounded and wound up working at the Soviet Hospital. "Conditions were really terrible. There were about three hundred patients and no medicine. Some had dreadful wounds invaded by maggots. There were about nine such unfortunates, and they were in awful pain, screaming, shouting and crying all the time. . . . When the Khmer Rouge saw a Chinese in dying condition, they would hit him with a stick until he was dead, then dump the body in a ditch on the hospital grounds. I saw about six people killed in this manner. . . . The patients with the maggots in their wounds, the Khmer Rouge took them from the hospital and threw them into the river."

Frequently during the first days after victory, the communists bragged that they were eliminating all prostitution in Cambodia, and they may have been right. At the Chamcar Khnor Temple, a kilometer outside Sisophon, a truck driver in late April stumbled upon one example of how this feat was achieved. He saw the crumpled bodies of about twenty young women. Each had been bludgeoned to death with blows on the back of the head. The truck driver knew some of the women as prostitutes and concluded that the rest were also.

The communists also killed some students, teachers and others classified as intellectuals for no apparent reason other than their education. Approximately 2,000 schoolteachers were incarcerated in a concentration camp established at Wat Ek monastery northwest of Battambang and another 1,000 or so interned at a camp near Kpop, northeast of the city. A driver for the communists who later escaped to Thailand claimed that in May he saw soldiers kill seventeen teachers from the Wat Ek camp with axes.

Expelled from Phnom Penh, civil servant Yen Savannary in early June was drafted to work on a road repair gang near the town of Maung Russei. An *Angka* supervisor, known as Comrade Puth, one morning

ordered all 120 members of the gang to assemble in a
field. An engineer named Mon was hauled forward,
pleading for his life. "Forgive me," he begged. "I
promise to live like an ordinary person from now on."
Impervious to the pleas, Comrade Puth instructed
soldiers to tie the engineer's hands, and they led him
away for shooting. The charge, as Yen understood it,
was that the engineer, because of his "high knowledge," was *ipso facto* a counterrevolutionary.

Available evidence suggests that in the first months
the pogrom against intellectuals was not executed as
rigorously and pervasively as that against military
officers and other "impure" elements. But it soon
became sufficiently widespread to convince educated
people that to survive, they must hide their education.
People spoke not of their learning but of their igno-
rance, not of their talents and accomplishments but of
their plainness and ineptitude.

If *Angka Loeu* adjudged an officer or civil servant
especially impure, then it might also consider his
wife and children so contaminated as to be beyond
redemption. And perhaps the most painful phase of
the purification program was the elimination of
women and children so classified.

The communists may or may not have learned that
Major Phim, one of the four known survivors of the
Mount Tippadei massacre, had escaped. But a few
days after the massacre a squad of twelve soldiers
came to his village home 22 kilometers southwest of
Battambang and arrested all family members present:
his wife, three children, a two-year-old granddaugh-
ter and a newborn grandson. Major Phim's thirteen-
year-old son, who was not at home at the time, subsequently told his father that they had killed all six,
including the baby.

In the village of Thmei, *Angka Loeu* uncovered a first lieutenant who had disguised himself. Five soldiers took him, his schoolteacher wife, their two teenage sons and two daughters, ages nine and seven, and stripped them naked. They herded the family through the village, beating them with a stick as if driving cattle. About a kilometer outside the village, they opened fire with AK-47 automatic rifles, killing all.

Fleeing to Thailand to avoid execution, a twenty-four-year-old officer, Nuth Peng, happened upon another deathly scene off an old road six kilometers west of Phnom Srok. "In a field some seventy meters away, there were about eighty bodies lying parallel to the road. About forty were men, some civilians and some soldiers. I could tell from their uniforms that some were officers. The rest were apparently the men's families—more than thirty women and a few children and old people. There was much blood on the back of the heads, so I assume that they had been clubbed to death. All had been dead about three or four days."

Angka Loeu, rightly or wrongly, identified many inhabitants of the village of Kauk Lon as former officers, customs officials and police agents. On or about April 20 troops marched the whole village population of some sixty families out of their huts and into Arak Bak Kar forest less than a kilometer away. As the people walked among the trees, machine-gun squads lying in ambush cut down the families—approximately 360 men, women, and children.

With the end of the war Sergeant Sreap Huot went home to his village, Bak Nim, 24 kilometers east of Samrong. A rice-growing community of about sixty people, Bak Nim had fervently supported the government, not out of a liking for Lon Nol but out of loathing for the Vietnamese with whom the communists were allied. Like Sreap, most of the young men in the village had volunteered for the army and for years fought the communists.

One evening, out of the darkness, a forty-three-man Khmer Rouge squad entered Bak Nim. The leader, a man of about thirty, announced that eight of the ten families were to move immediately to another village. The two families left behind were the only ones whose members did not include a soldier.

Escorting the frightened group of about fifty villagers a short distance from Bak Nim, the communists dispensed with their resettlement fiction. "Now tell the truth," a soldier shouted at Sreap. "You were a Lon Nol soldier."

The squad had its M-16 rifles pointed. There was nothing the villagers could do. "Yes," Sreap admitted, "I was a soldier, but I wasn't an officer."

"High rank or low rank, it doesn't matter," the soldier said. "*Angka* says *all* soldiers must die. We have to kill them!"

Seizing the villagers, all but the smallest children, the communists tied their arms behind their backs with nylon rope. They even trussed up Sreap's recently widowed mother, who, despite her bonds, was forced to carry her two-year-old daughter as best she could. The villagers were then blindfolded, lashed together and marched in a long line into the jungle.

For what seemed to Sreap about one and one-half hours, the communist escort forced the group forward. The ex-sergeant's blindfold had not been tied tightly, and he was able to see a bizarre parade. Ahead were several soldiers carrying flaming resin torches. Then came the prisoners, strangely silent. The greater part of the communist squad brought up the rear. The rustle of undergrowth and the sobbing of children were the only sounds to be heard.

Suddenly, at the head of the column, commotion developed, and new noises—a series of dull thuds—began. Sreap was pushed to the ground, and a soldier swung at the back of his neck with a wooden club. A blinding pain . . . and Sreap lost consciousness.

About an hour later he came to. In the darkness, Sreap's would-be executioner had apparently miscalculated by an inch or so, the club striking his shoulders instead of his spinal cord.

After lying still for some time, the ex-sergeant concluded that the communists had departed. His arms were no longer tied; the soldiers apparently had taken all their nylon rope with them. Pushing aside three corpses which had fallen on top of him, Sreap struggled to his feet and began an anguished search for his family—his mother, his nineteen-year-old wife, his six-year-old brother and two other sisters, ages four and three.

But no moon shone through the jungle canopy, and blackness surrounded him. All around corpses filled the air with the sickly scent of fresh blood. Here and there among adult bodies he stumbled on the remains of one of the village's infants. Unable to find any of his relatives and finally convinced he was the only survivor, he staggered toward Thailand and crossed the border four days later.

One night in mid-May a squad of communist soldiers appeared at Khal Kabei village in Thmar Puok District. "Stay close to your homes tonight," they told puzzled villagers. "It could be dangerous for you if you travel beyond Khal Kabei." The people were even

more mystified by the sight of communist soldiers
driving past on a tractor towing a trailer carrying
about forty women aged between eighteen and
twenty-five.

As the dawn came and the villagers left their houses
to work in the rice paddies, they discovered why the
Khmer Rouge had wanted the night to themselves.
About 160 meters along a cart track east of Khal Kabei
were the remains of the forty young women. "They
had been buried up to the necks," said one of the
villagers. "You could see only their heads—in a line
along the track, about five meters apart." Down the
long and grisly row, blood mingled with the early-
morning dew. Each of the women had been stabbed in
the throat.

For more than a week, as the heads became swollen
with putrefaction and the smell of death permeated
the village, the Khmer Rouge refused to let Khal Kabei
arrange a proper burial. *Kael American kael Lon Nol*
(the scurf of the Americans and Lon Nol), the soldiers
called them. "You don't have to worry about them."
From the girls' appearance, especially the careful
grooming of their long hair, the villagers guessed that
they were the wives and daughters of officers and
senior civil servants. The tractor that brought them
came from the direction of Mongkol Borei, the town
in which a month previously so many men in these
categories had said good-bye to their unworried, un-
knowing families and gone off gaily to greet Prince
Sihanouk.

On April 27 at Mongkol Borei *Angka Loeu* further
"purified" the population. A communist commander
named Prom ordered a squad of fifteen young soldiers

to punish some former government officials "because they worked for Lon Nol." Led by an officer called Taan, who was in his early thirties, the soldiers rounded up ten civil servants together with their wives and children, about sixty people in all. They bound the hands of each behind the back, forced them aboard a truck and at about 5 P.M. drove them some 3 kilometers out of town to a banana plantation adjoining Banteay Neang village.

Weeping, sobbing, begging for their lives, the prisoners were pushed into a clearing among the banana trees, then formed into a ragged line, the terrified mothers and children clustering around each head of the family. With military orderliness, the communists thrust each official forward one at a time and forced him to kneel between two soldiers armed with bayonet-tipped AK-47 rifles. The soldiers then stabbed the victim simultaneously, one through the chest and the other through the back. Family by family, the communists pressed the slaughter, moving methodically down the line. As each man lay dying, his anguished, horror-struck wife and children were dragged up to his body. The women, forced to kneel, also received the simultaneous bayonet thrusts. The children and babies, last to die, were stabbed where they stood.

It had been very noisy among the banana trees when the families arrived. Attracted by the uproar, villagers rushed from Banteay Neang and, when they saw what was happening moved just as quickly away. As the bodies piled higher, there were fewer prisoners shouting, and as the last child was dispatched, an eyewitness, thirty-five-year-old Ith Thaim, whom the

Khmer Rouge had drafted to drive the truck, remembers that a terrible stillness settled over the plantation, the Khmer Rouge saying nothing, "the blood like water on the grass."

The hush was broken as the soldiers, most in their late teens, were being driven back to Mongkol Borei in the gathering dusk. "That old man," said one of the Khmer Rouge. "Those first two stabs should have been enough, but we had to go back to him two or three times. He took a long time to die."

A twenty-two-year-old Khmer Rouge soldier, Penh Choerm, in May was assigned to guard former military personnel and some of their families held captive at a pagoda in Sisophon. Interned were about 150 men, 30 women, 10 boys and 10 girls. Penh thought the prisoners were fed and treated well, and to him the atmosphere at the temple seemed almost pleasant.

At eight o'clock one morning four or five buses parked in front of the temple. An officer summoned the men and boys and informed them they were being transferred to work in rice fields. With Penh along as one of the escorts, the buses started north on the road to Svay Chek. Barely half a kilometer outside Sisophon, they halted, and the prisoners were ordered to disembark. A large number of soldiers—Penh estimated 200—rushed from the woods and surrounded the buses. As the men and boys stepped off, the soldiers grabbed them and tied their hands with scarves or nylon cords used for hammocks. They then lashed the prisoners together in groups of three or four and marched them into a rice field about 50 meters from the road. Some thirty armed sentries were posted on the periphery of the field, and in the distance a few peasants were plowing.

The commander of the soldiers, a Comrade Bao, waved his right hand down in a cutting motion three times. Instantly the soldiers began bayoneting and stabbing the doomed in the back. Some of the victims tried to run, only to be cut down by automatic rifle fire. The children were clubbed to death, and Penh saw the faces of some smashed in.

Two boys, one about ten, the other about five years old, ran hysterically in a circle around their father, who was being bayoneted to death. Penh remembers the scene. "Khmer Rouge soldiers chased them. They were laughing at them. They chased after them as if they were chasing ducks or chickens. And the soldiers around laughed too. They caught the boys and beat them to death."

After the screams and moans ceased, Penh asked a soldier, "How did you feel when you were killing them? Were you afraid?"

"The first time I was a little afraid," the soldier answered. "But after two or three it's easy."

Now the temple back in Sisophon was empty of prisoners. While their husbands and fathers were dying, the women and girls had been taken away, so Penh was told, to be slaughtered by female Khmer Rouge soldiers.

A CHILD'S
JOURNEY

The evacuations of the cities, like the early massacres, were accomplished with a dispatch and efficiency that suggested thorough planning. The occupation troops knew, after the first day or so, exactly what to do, and their actions were well coordinated. However, once the urban population had been tumbled out of the cities, no planning or coordination was evident, and communist soldiers herding the outcasts along the highways often seemed as confused as their captives. They simply pointed people in a given direction and at gunpoint kept them moving, without specifying a destination. A few kilometers down the highway or road, other soldiers might drive the same people off in another direction, again without explanation. Perhaps *Angka Loeu* reasoned that the purposes of social disintegration would be best served by an unplanned, random scattering of the people rather than by orderly relocation. Whatever the reason, while the bonfires of Cambodian culture burned in the desolated cities and the knives of *Angka Loeu* carved out undesirables, between 3,000,000 and 4,000,000 people marched and wandered chaotically through the countryside toward nowhere. Among themselves, Cambodians swept into this great exodus soon referred to themselves as the "people of the Emigration."

On her second day in the Emigration the beautiful fourteen-year-old child from Phnom Penh, Tevi Rosa, awakened amid the dead in the house at the edge of the city where she and her family spent the night. Her uncle and leader of the party, architect Ly Bun Heng, had heard that to the south, hunger and death were widespread. So that morning, April 24, they took a road eastward toward Vietnam, but at a bridge a guard barred their way and motioned them southward. "Comrade, let us pass the bridge," Ly said. The guard shoved a rifle into his stomach, and Ly instantly backed away, sensing that another word might be fatal.

Not far from the bridge Ly spotted an abandoned jeep he knew well. It belonged to Rosa's father, the colonel who had entrusted his family to him the night before Phnom Penh fell. To Ly, the empty jeep signified that his brother-in-law probably was dead, and consequently he said nothing about it to the rest of the family.

They took turns pushing Ly's red Fiat, packed with rice, canned food, clothing, a portable stove, cooking fuel, a transistor radio and sundry personal belongings. Rosa had put her schoolbooks, including algebra and geometry texts, in the car, sure that wherever they went, she would continue her studies. At checkpoints every few miles on the road, soldiers searched bypassers and confiscated whichever possessions interested them. Therefore, Ly repacked the car, putting valuables and some food under the seats. The family also hid jewelry and gold on their persons.

Rosa saw people still pushing hospital beds bearing patients and felt very sorry for them. The wheels swiveled constantly, making it difficult to propel the beds forward, and some of the sick begged for relief from their pain. The farther they advanced, the more empty hospital beds there were by the roadside, and each told Rosa somebody else had died. Death had become so commonplace, though, that it no longer shocked. Her mind had anesthetized itself against the sight of the bodies of little children, women and men, infested by worms, pecked at by birds, bloated by the sun into inhuman shape. She wanted to cry, but as she had learned the first day of the march, tears no longer would come.

Ashamed because she perspired constantly and was so dirty, Rosa worried because no one said where they should or could go or how long they must trek onward. She worried about her mother, whose pretty face had changed into a fixed mask of sadness. Most of all, she worried about her adored father, and throughout the days she scanned the road, hoping by the hour to catch sight of his jeep.

The family walked southward for several days along the Bassac River through forsaken, ghostly villages, sleeping in deserted pagodas or huts or under a large piece of plastic with which Ly used to cover his car. The only source of water was the dirty river on which floated oil, dead leaves, other debris and occasionally a body. Looking at the green algae and dark particles in her first cup of water, Rosa thought she could never drink it. The searing heat generated such thirst that she soon surmounted revulsion by closing her eyes and swallowing the foul-tasting liquid in big gulps.

At a roadblock on the outskirts of Saang, a village 48 kilometers south of Phnom Penh, the family was subjected to a seventh search. Here the soldiers were confiscating all books and papers, which they threw into a fire blazing nearby. They made Rosa give up her little diary notebook, and she watched as they tossed it and her schoolbooks into the flames. They even burned the identification papers of Ly, his younger brother and eighty-eight-year-old father.

"Comrade, now that we have lost our identity, how will you recognize us?" Ly asked.

"Don't call me comrade!" the soldier said truculently. "Only brothers-in-arms may call us comrade. Call me brother or uncle or whatever you wish, but not comrade!" The soldier was maybe sixteen.

Along with hundreds of other outcasts from Phnom Penh, Rosa and her relatives stopped for the night at a school in Saang, and there all were summoned to a meeting presided over by three young peasant soldiers. "All of you come from Phnom Penh, and we want to make it clear that you should forget about returning there," the one in charge began.

"All of you will work in the fields, for we must think of production now, and our only production is agriculture. Those of you who want to stay in the area of Saang and work here can go to the *Angka Loeu* office tomorrow morning to put your names down. Those who wish to go farther south can continue your route tomorrow. But everybody will work in the fields."

There were gasps of incredulity. A tiny woman,

whom Ly knew as the wealthy owner of a Phnom
Penh plywood store, quickly stood up. Two of her
children were studying in England and two in Hong
Kong, and she frantically asked, "What should I do
about my children who are abroad? I have to send
them money for their upkeep every month. How
should I do this now?"

"I wouldn't know about that," the soldier replied.
"What I do know is that for the construction of our
new Cambodia we don't need people who went to
school and know foreign languages."

"All right," the mother shouted, "but meanwhile,
how can I get money to my children?"

"You shouldn't have sent your children abroad in
the first place," the soldier answered.

A man wanted to know what would happen to his
home and other property in Phnom Penh. "Everything
belongs to *Angka Loeu* now," he was told.

As more and more women wept and people exclaimed their disbelief to each other, the meeting
degenerated into bedlam. The three soldiers abruptly
walked out, leaving behind a crowd stupefied by this,
the first explicit, official explanation of the future.

Until now most people had accepted the communist explanation that evacuation of the cities was
temporary. Even Ly believed that the momentarily
expected return of Prince Sihanouk would restore
sanity to the land. Any society, he reasoned, would
require physicians, engineers, architects, technicians. This need, coupled with his personal ties to
Sihanouk, would ensure him and his relatives a place
in Phnom Penh, he thought. Terrible as the agonies of
the Emigration had been, they until now seemed to be
a transient curse that eventually would be lifted. But

with the announcement that henceforth everybody without exception would labor in the fields, never to return to the cities, Ly could foresee only enduring enslavement.

The next morning the one remaining liberty apparently accorded them, the freedom to continue southward, was taken away. Barely 5 kilometers down the road from Saang a patrol halted them, and the leader said they must settle nearby because areas to the south had become overcrowded. Pointing to the adjacent village of Samphan, he commanded, "Find yourself a place to stay until we get you organized."

They moved into a rickety house on piles in Samphan with three other Phnom Penh families and, pending their unknown disposition by *Angka Loeu*, busied themselves hunting wild fruit, berries, edible leaves and field crabs. Rosa winced at the sight of three small children living in the house because they were covered with huge, ugly blisters, many of which had burst and become infected. A physician among the exiles told their father, a banker, that the blisters resulted from heat and inadequate hygiene and advised that the children urgently needed antibiotics. Together with the father, Ly visited the village chief to plead for medicine. "Give me their names, and I will tell *Angka Loeu*, " the chief said. "*Angka Loeu* will decide whether they should have medicine." None was forthcoming, and Rosa continued to be haunted by the almost continuous crying of the children, whose torment worsened daily.

The plight of an aged, shrunken Chinese woman whom Rosa saw each day saddened her even more. In the chaotic congestion of the exodus the tiny woman had become separated from her family, probably because she could not keep up the pace demanded by soldiers who periodically goaded the exiles to move faster. Utterly lost, she planted herself on the road through the village, sleeping on the open ground at night, weeping and watching throughout the day, hoping that by chance her family would pass by and reclaim her. People gave her food, but she refused to leave the road, so fearful was she of missing her family. Looking at her, Rosa thought now that death was indeed preferable to some forms of life.

On the fifth day in the village soldiers directed the people to assemble at a pagoda on the riverbank preparatory to proceeding to the final destination *Angka Loeu* had chosen for them. Ly purposely waited a couple of hours and then, alone and on foot, threaded his way through the weeds along the river to reconnoiter. From the pagoda, families were being ferried across the river in small boats. They had to leave behind cars and all belongings except the few they could carry in their hands.

All the way from Phnom Penh, Ly and his family had pushed the car, turning on the engine only when ascending steep hills, in order to save the few gallons of gas in the tank for an emergency. Confronted with its imminent loss, he decided to use the car while he still could and attempt to take the family somewhere, anywhere less foreboding.

They slipped out of Samphan in a fierce midmorning rainstorm and drove until Ly had to slow down at a large village formerly known as Kohr Thom. There soldiers with pointed rifles told them they would go no farther. All would stay in the village and work in the fields, and they would give the car to *Angka Loeu*. Before parking his Fiat for the last time, Ly removed the hidden food and valuables and in a little gesture of defiance inverted the spark plugs.

The communists had occupied Kohr Thom long ago, retitled it Village No. 3 and routed the original inhabitants. Every three months or so they brought in new residents and expelled the old, possibly to keep the population in disarray and inhibit coalescence of any opposition. As a consequence, no one had any incentive to maintain anything, and the place was in a state of dreary delapidation.

Many newcomers from Phnom Penh corraled in the village were sleeping under trees. But Ly, after making inquiries and approaching a person known as Comrade Aunt, arranged something better for his family. An illiterate woman with a protuberant jaw, Comrade Aunt reminded Ly and Rosa of a duck because she walked with her feet pointed outward and talked in a high-pitched, quacking voice. Her son was the village chieftain, and her daughters served in the militia, so she had been given a house of her own and authority over women of the village. In return for tacit agreement that Ly and his relatives would perform chores for her, she consented to let them live under her house, which stood on stilts. Considering themselves fortunate, they settled into a space about six meters long and 3 meters wide. It did not seem to matter that their abode was shared by two communal oxen.

All the family, with the exception of Rosa's mother, who suffered an attack of acute asthma, and Ly's elderly father, immediately were put to work. They rose at 4:30 A.M., walked to surrounding fields at 6:30 and remained there until 5 P.M. Rosa and the other females dug irrigation ditches under the supervision of Com-

rade Aunt. Ly, together with other professionals from
Phnom Penh, including a physician, pulled weeds
from rice paddies.

Each working person received from *Angka Loeu* a
weekly ration consisting only of 500 grams of captured American rice brought in from Phnom Penh, four
kilograms of corn and 100 grams of salt, and hunger
forced everyone into a struggle for more food. Ly
found himself trying to outgrab other men for snails
that turned up in the weeds. Rosa, taught all her
young life to regard stealing as an unthinkable sin,
pilfered mangoes and other fruit from the trees—a
serious offense in light of the endlessly repeated
warning that every tree, every piece of fruit, every
stick of wood belonged to *Angka Loeu*. Her thirteen-
year-old brothers, assigned to husk corn, rolled up the
legs of their pants to create cuffs into which they
dropped grains of corn. Intermittently, they excused
themselves to go behind a tree to hide the accumulated corn, and at night they delivered it all to the
family. The corn had to be soaked in water and
pounded in a mortar before it could be cooked. There
was only one mortar in Village No. 3, and on some
evenings Rosa or other family members stood in line
until 2 A.M. waiting to use it.

A middle-aged man quartered near Comrade Aunt's
house openly complained, "They make us work like
dogs, and we don't even have enough to eat." Two
days later the man failed to come home from the
fields, and his concerned wife asked Ly to accompany
her to see the village chief.

"Maybe he said something *Angka Loeu* does not
like," the chief suggested. "In that case, *Angka Loeu*
came to fetch him, to educate him."

Accustomed to dealing successfully with men of power, Ly cultivated the chief, stopping by when he could to drink a glass of palm wine with him. The chief was a coarse peasant prejudiced against urban dwellers. At best, though, he was a halfhearted convert to communism, and he had a kind of rough sense of humor. As Ly was to discover, he also was capable of discreet kindness, and the two got along well.

Relations with Comrade Aunt, however, deteriorated. In the interests of the family, Ly tried to oblige her by sweeping floors, gathering wood and cleaning up ox dung. But the more he did, the more she demanded, and one day she curtly ordered him to go to the river and bring back two heavy buckets of water. Partially because of a weak back, partially because he felt her petty tyranny should not be allowed to grow, Ly just as curtly refused. Thereafter Comrade Aunt turned into such a spiteful spy that if the family wished to talk privately, they spoke French.

Walking to and from the river to bathe, Rosa each day passed an encampment housing disabled communist soldiers. Some were without arms, legs or eyes; all were grievously and permanently maimed. Rosa pitied their suffering and mutilation, yet she was repulsed by their filth. They were so dirty that she could not discern where their Ho Chi Minh sandals ended and their ankles began. Always when they looked covetously or shouted suggestive remarks at her, she turned away, shuddering.

One night the village chief came to see his mother, Comrade Aunt, and the two sat on the front steps with another man. Lying under the house a few meters away, Rosa and her mother could not help hearing them. The chief revealed there was to be a grand festival celebrating the birth of the new Cambodia. Before the entire village all the girls from Phnom Penh would be lined up and each made to dance so as to display herself. After the exhibition each invalid from the convalescent camp would be allowed to pick a wife from among the girls. Any girls left over would be taken by war heroes. All the Phnom Penh girls that same evening would be married off in a mass wedding staged by *Angka Loeu*.

"Just think, these guys have not had a woman in five years!" exclaimed the chief. "They paid for victory with their blood, and the weddings will be their reward."

"*Angka Loeu* is quite right," Comrade Aunt concurred.

Relishing the prospects, the chief and the other, unknown man ribaldly and explicitly talked about how the decadent city girls who had lived in luxury throughout the war deserved what was about to happen to them.

"Do you hear? Do you hear?" Rosa's mother whispered. Trembling, Rosa did not answer. When the chief left, her mother again whispered, "I am going to have a talk with Uncle Heng."

Rosa thought of all the sacrifices her parents had made to prepare her for a life founded on gentility, tolerance and compassion. She thought of all she had seen since peace came. She thought of the spiritual defilement and legalized rape awaiting her, of what life might be like as the slave of an unknown, unwashed, unwanted man. Again, she was shaking. Now, though, she trembled not with fear but with hatred.

News of the impending mass wedding leaped through the village overnight, and the next afternoon, coming back from the fields, Ly was astounded by the reactions of girls he overheard talking about it. Soberly and calmly, they were discussing the most effective methods of suicide. One contended the preferable method was to slash the arteries in the wrists. Another argued that hanging was best, "provided that the knot is at the back of the neck; otherwise, it won't work." It was Rosa who coldly proposed that no girl commit suicide until each had managed to kill her new husband. Quickly the proposal became a murder pact, and the girls began a wide-ranging discussion of the best ways to kill, given the means likely to be available to them on their wedding night.

The evening before, Ly's sister had beseeched him to try to spirit Rosa out of Cambodia, whatever the risk to him and her. The communists already had made clear that anyone caught attempting to flee the country would be killed, and Ly calculated that the chances of escaping alive were small. Nevertheless, having heard Rosa, a fourteen-year-old child, earnestly plotting murder and suicide, he decided to try.

Analyzing the possibilities of escape, Ly could not conceive how any Cambodian reasonably could expect to evade all the checkpoints and patrols of *Angka Loeu*. What, he speculated, if one were to become Vietnamese? He spoke Vietnamese fluently; Rosa not a word. However, there lived in Village No. 3 the large Catholic Vietnamese family of a former Phnom Penh jeweler named Dak. His nine children included three desirable daughters—Bernadette, Elizabeth and Alexandra—who also would be gifts for the cripples. If Dak and all his children came along, Rosa might be able to mingle with them and pass unnoticed as Vietnamese.

Dak was reluctant. He had left three safes full of

jewels, representing the accumulated wealth of a lifetime, back in Phnom Penh, and he feared that unless he recovered them, his family would be ruined. Through persistence, Ly ultimately convinced him that his property, his business and all chances of ever returning to Phnom Penh were irretrievably gone. Once Dak agreed to Ly's scheme, he became a committed and efficient conspirator.

Never during his chats with the village chief had Ly disclosed that his wife and children were in Paris. Instead, he sorrowfully explained that he had lost them in the first day of the exodus. Feigning excitement, Ly now reported to the chief that he had just heard his wife and children had been seen a few days before at a pagoda some distance to the south. Could he have permission to go find them?

"Controls are not very strict yet," the chief said. "But they will be very soon, and you might not be able to move about then. When you have found your family, you can come back here."

Casually, Ly mentioned that he would like to take Rosa along, and instantly the chief was suspicious, so much so that the whole venture seemed in jeopardy. Thinking quickly, Ly said, man to man, that he required Rosa as a cook, and the chief was mollified.

One by one, so as to not alert Comrade Aunt, Rosa and her mother brought possessions out of hiding and prepared the escape kit: 10 kilograms of rice, 10 liters of cooking fuel, some streptomycin and other medication, a plate and a knife. Rosa's mother sewed jewelry and two thin sheets of pure gold into a pair of Rosa's panties. For the journey Ly used a bicycle which *Angka Loeu* had tagged No. 1640.

The morning of the departure Rosa's mother said,

"You must be strong at all times. Remember, your presence is making Heng's escape much more difficult than if he were alone. So don't add to his burden." Her younger brothers, wide-eyed upon seeing that she was leaving, asked where she was going. "Don't ask me," Rosa answered. "I'm going far, and I have to leave you all. Take good care of Mummy." As they loaded their gear on bicycle No. 1640, Rosa's mother, knowing she was seeing her child for the last time, wept silently.

Rendezvousing with the Dak family outside the village, Ly and Rosa assumed their new Vietnamese identities. Ly became Tran Van Hao, and Rosa his daughter, Tran Thi Hua—"lotus flower." Rosa was to avoid speaking to anyone outside the escape party lest she betray her true nationality. But if she had to talk, her orders were to speak in backwoods Khmer, the language of the Khmer Rouge she so often had heard in the countryside. Tanned during the long hours in sun-drenched fields, they had long since lost their city pallor, and they tried to adopt the mannerisms as well as the appearance of peasants.

The journey began badly. Less than a kilometer from Village No. 3, a guard obdurately refused to permit them to cross a bridge over the Bassac River. A few minutes before they arrived, the bridge was open. But the guard had just received a command to let nobody pass, and no amount of talk about repatriation of Vietnamese could dissuade him.

Nobody in Ly's group had a written authorization to travel, so they fled southward along the river, looking for another crossing. The sky blackened, and amid thunder, rain poured down so torrentially they could scarcely see. They came to a small village about noon, and the Daks and Rosa rested under a house while Ly scouted the waterfront in search of a boat.

A man told him there was only one boat in the village, and it belonged to *Angka Loeu*. Speaking with the thick Vietnamese accent, Ly suggested that if the boat could be made available long enough to transport thirteen foreigners to the other side of the river, the man would be rewarded with a liter of cooking fuel. The villager professed powerlessness to help until Ly enlarged the proffered bribe by mentioning a magic word, "medicine." With that, the villager promised to bring the boat quickly.

Waiting beneath a tree, Ly saw Rosa running through the rain toward him. "Uncle Heng, you have been recognized!" she said. "I heard a man in the house say to his wife, 'There's Ly, the architect. He makes piles of money. You could burn twenty corpses with his banknotes." In danger of losing their new identities and thereby their lives, Ly and Rosa, together with Dak, his wife and their nine children, hurried into the boat, carrying bicycle No. 1640, a Dak family bicycle and their supplies.

Across the river they walked eastward toward Vietnam in the unabating rain. Rosa was soaked and in agony. The jewelry and gold sewn into her underpants chafed from the outset and wore her flesh so raw that each step was a small torture. Guilt also pained her. Back in the village her brothers were working all day, serving Comrade Aunt at night, looking thinner and thinner. Her mother, upon recovery from the asthma, would also be a serf in the fields. Her beloved father had vanished. She remembered how she had bossed and quarreled with her younger brothers, how she had failed, so she thought, to express her love and gratitude to her parents. She longed to be with them all again, to hug them all, to make amends. She realized now that she would never have the chance. Lagging behind so no one would see, Rosa cried for the first time since leaving Phnom Penh.

Toward dusk they reached a village whose chief was part Vietnamese. With Ly and Rosa keeping in the background, Dak and his oldest daughter, Elizabeth, asked if they could stay the night. The chief, under orders to detain all strangers moving toward the border, was skeptical and hostile. Elizabeth, an appealing woman of twenty-five, engaged him in conversation. "Do you have children? I hope they are well," she said, knowing they almost certainly were not because sickness was prevalent everywhere. The children indeed were ill, and the chief, who was very worried about them, gladly took the medicine Elizabeth offered. Thus bribed, he showed them to a hut for the night. "Leave tomorrow morning at three o'clock before I'm up," he said. "If I see you, I'll have to arrest you and make you stay here." Dak was so eager to get away that he awakened everybody at half past midnight.

About ten that morning soldiers stopped them as they attempted to transit another village. They explained to the chief who came to interrogate them that they as Vietnamese had been granted permission to return to their homeland. The chief was enraged. "Why do those fellows up the road do such a bad job?" he wanted to know. "They have the same orders as I have—to arrest everyone trying to pass. They're incapable of a decent job!" In apparent disgust at the incompetence of his colleagues, he waved the party on. However, he had second thoughts.

When Ly, Rosa and the Daks walked into the next village, he was waiting for them, leaning on his bicycle in the middle of the road. He brusquely directed them to an empty hut and announced, "First, I'm going to search your luggage. And then you will just have to settle here and work in the field like everybody else."

Going through Dak's bag, he noticed some prayer books, small statues of Christ and a cross, and he pocketed them all. He obviously was fascinated by a yellowish volcanic stone that looked like gold, so Dak told him it was his. Like a child with a toy, he played with a small directory whose pages at the press of a button popped open at the letter indicated. Elizabeth, to whom the directory belonged, invited him to keep it. Discovering the medicine, the chief remarked that one of his children was suffering from malaria. Quickly Bernadette, who had been a medical student, gave him quinine and instructed him about dosages. Again the medicine worked. "First, I have to leave this village," said the chief. "If you go before I'm out of sight, I'll have to arrest you." As soon as he pedaled away, Ly, Rosa and the Daks fled.

In two more villages they rescued themselves from captivity or worse with bribes of medicine. And in the large village of Leuk Dek on the Mekong, Bernadette, by ministering to a young girl feverish with malaria, induced the girl's uncle to take them 11 kilometers downriver by boat to the village of Peam Kleang, or Village No. 1 as *Angka Loeu* titled it.

The village was crowded with Vietnamese, and the first person they met there was a former first secretary of the South Vietnamese embassy in Phnom Penh. Accepting them as Vietnamese, he led them to an old hut where they could stay. Shortly after they settled, the village chief, a belligerent Vietnamese-speaking woman with a raucous voice, arrived to put them on the list of people who had entered the village that day. Rosa, with her beautiful typically Khmer face, immediately aroused her suspicions.

"Are you the daughter of this man?" she snapped at Rosa in Vietnamese while pointing at Ly.

"Yes," one of the Daks' daughters quickly interjected. "That's her father."

Finishing recording the names, the chief again eyed Rosa, who was wearing a traditional Khmer sarong rather than the wide black pants and white blouse customary among Vietnamese girls. "What are you doing?" she loudly demanded.

One of the Dak girls bobbed up beside the chief. "Oh," she said, "Thi Hua is cooking our meal."

The female chieftain departed, but soon she was back, determined to verify her amorphous suspicions. She bluntly asked the Daks if any Cambodians were hiding among them, and the question frightened all, for they knew if Ly and Rosa were discovered, all would be taken to *Angka Loeu*. Desperately they fell back on the tactics that had served in every other crisis of the flight. From her bag Mrs. Dak offered the chieftain two pieces of fabric, and somebody made an allusion to medicine. Distracted by the prospect of medicine, the chief asked if they had any effective against diarrhea. Bernadette gave her some and as an added gesture handed her some salt. Having accepted the bribes, the woman grudgingly said she would do her best to secure authorization from the district chief for them to journey on to Vietnam.

As she left, she saw Rosa climbing the stairs of a hut

nearby. Making a last, halfhearted attempt to solve the mystery Rosa presented to her, she yelled, "Where have you been?"

Alexandra Dak popped her head out of the opening at the top of the stairs. "At the river," Rosa's friend yelled back in Vietnamese. "Washing clothes."

That afternoon the woman returned, shouting as she approached. "You can leave tomorrow, but you must leave your bicycles behind. And don't go before dawn. It must be light enough for the patrols to recognize you. Otherwise they might shoot."

At daybreak the thirteen "Vietnamese" left in fear that the chief might at any moment arbitrarily reverse her decision or that some other malign caprice might arise to block their way to the border about 32 kilometers away. Without their bicycles, they carried the remaining supplies on a stretcher made out of bamboo and fabric. Anxiety impelled them to walk all day without pause until darkness forced them to stop on the bank of the Mekong. Despite their exhaustion, tension and hordes of mosquitoes made sleep impossible.

The next day they headed south, and the closer to the border they advanced, the faster they tried to walk. They began to throw away the belongings whose weight slowed them—buckets for water, their fuel, bottles, a hammer, then even nails. About noon they approached the last *Angka Loeu* checkpoint, which was notorious for searches and inquisitions. But now their luck was holding. The guards that morning had searched a large number of refugees and, pleased with a good day's work, had taken time off to eat lunch at a small pagoda. Ly, Rosa and the Daks were able to slip past along the riverbank unseen.

Near the border the road dwindled to a trail, then into a narrow path. South Vietnam three weeks before had fallen to the communists, and in the distance, near the intersection of the Mekong and the Vietnamese border, they could see red flags. Suddenly they felt themselves so physically and emotionally depleted that they could not go on. They rested about an hour, trying to summon strength to traverse the last few hundred meters.

"Welcome!" cheerfully shouted a Vietnamese official. Taking them for Vietnamese repatriates, he curiously and sympathetically asked about the travail in Cambodia. Upon hearing their brief summary of what had occurred since April 17, he shook his head. "Well, anyway, that is all over for you now. No more searches. You are free."

Ly remembers the moment vividly. "At the border village right after we crossed into Vietnam, Mr. Dak met a former worker of his. Both were delighted, and the worker invited all of us to his house. He gave us iced coffee. As I savored it, I remembered the last iced coffee I had—on April 17 in a restaurant on the Central Market Square in Phnom Penh. It seemed centuries ago."

Thinking of all she had seen and lost, Rosa could say nothing. She was a traumatized child, forever changed by the hideousness she had experienced. Still, Rosa was one of the lucky ones.

V

INTO
THE JUNGLES

On the five national highways leading out of Phnom Penh, the temperature in those last days of April rose at midday above 100 degrees Fahrenheit and dropped at night below 65 degrees. The dry season now ending had parched the flatlands and evaporated the rice paddies, leaving behind stagnant, fetid pools and depleted ponds increasingly fouled by excrement and bodies. Sudden daytime cloudbursts and frigid evening downpours harshened the environment. And the 3,000,000 outcasts from Phnom Penh—slowly trudging the highways in long, ragged, congested columns, scorched by the sun, whipped by arid winds, guarded and goaded by the guns of *Angka Loeu*—were almost wholly exposed to the elements.

No stores of potable water, no stocks of food, no shelter of any kind had been prepared for them. They slept wherever they could: sometimes in empty huts, in forsaken pagodas, in abandoned schools or under trees; frequently in the open fields and ditches. Along some stretches of the highways, trucks did haphazardly distribute small quantities of American rice brought from Phnom Penh, but most families received none. As people exhausted the food they brought with them, malnutrition compounded the debilitating effects of dehydration.

Exiles shunted onto routes near rivers were more fortunate. But even here conditions were grim. Pharmacist Kyheng Savang on April 26 found himself about 6 kilometers outside Phnom Penh in a vast conglomeration marching north on Highway 5 parallel to the Mekong. "At twilight we settled on the left side of the road, set up our mosquito nets and slept all night. Next morning my sister wanted to know if I had slept well because we had practically planted our mosquito nets on fresh graves. Bodies must have been buried there just before we arrived.

"We walked practically all day, still in the company of hundreds of thousands of people. We walked over two bodies in the road, just as thousands must have done before us. They were flat like pancakes. I wondered what had happened to my compatriots.

"We spent the next two nights beneath a 105 millimeter gun on the banks of the Mekong. The gun was brand-new, still wrapped in its plastic hood. It made for excellent shelter. As I was taking a bath in the Mekong, the body of a soldier floated past. Everybody else fled; I went on washing myself.

"After two nights we were ordered to leave, always along the Mekong. The road was still as jammed as ever. People were still pushing hospital beds, all sorts of vehicles and homemade carts. Some of the carts had wheels carved out of a solid piece of wood with an ordinary knife. Few of them were round. They jolted and bumped along, often making grating, squeaky noises. Atop this undercarriage was usually a structure made of wooden crates or boards and branches nailed together any old way. Very often old grandparents who could not walk anymore were sitting in these carts, together with sacks of rice and other belongings, while the rest of the family was pushing.

"We spent the following night in an almost completely destroyed pagoda along with thousands of people. I figured we had about one square meter of space for three people. Conditions were abominable. People cooked their rice between the head of one and the feet of another person. Smoke from the cookers was drifting over us. I thought that if I spent a week in this place, I was sure to catch tuberculosis.

"There were thousands of abandoned cars in the area. Many of them had no wheels left. The refugees took them to build pushcarts. Owners of Mercedes and other expensive cars were trying to swap them for bicycles. A bicycle does not need any gas. My sister bought a little cart. Its wheels were made of 105 millimeter shell casings; the top was an old wooden crate. My sister gave the owner two gold rings and a gold necklace for it, a total value of almost five hundred dollars. Her expensive little cart broke down after about five kilometers and had to be abandoned.

"We trekked on northward all the way to Prek Kdam. On the way, we asked Khmer Rouge soldiers for rice, and their answer was always the same: 'Ask Angka. Angka will give you rice.' But since nobody knew who or where was Angka, we received no rice.

"At Prek Kdam the refugees had to cross the

Mekong. There was one ferry, run by the Khmer Rouge. People were waiting their turn in the most terrible conditions. There was no village, no trees, not even shrubs. Just an empty plain. The temperature was a hundred and five degrees with a nasty wind blowing about clouds of dust. People were trying to protect themselves against the sun with wooden boards, mosquito nets, pieces of plastic, anything they could find. It often rained at night."

Predictably and inevitably, death thrived in such circumstances. The most innocent Cambodians, the very young and the very old, were the first to die. In the crush on the highways, adults and children slaked their thirst in roadside ditches. Consequently, acute dysentery racked bodies already weakened by hunger and fatigue. After the children, the elderly succumbed, then pregnant mothers, then middle-aged men and women accustomed to sedentary life. Frequently troops assigned to keep the multitudes moving refused to allow people to pause long enough to bury the beloved. The poignant keening of bereaved families driven at gunpoint away from the bodies of a child, grandparent, husband or wife deepened the misery pervading the highways.

Prevented by the abruptness of his forced departure from taking along medicine from the pharmacy, Kyheng Savang watched helplessly all one night as a seven-year-old boy died agonizingly of acute dehydration brought on by dysentery. Frightened of the communist soldiers, the family had walked continuously all that day, even though around noon the temperature soared to an unbearable height. Unable to stand the thirst, the boy and his younger brother and sister had drunk from a puddle. By morning the seven-year-old was dead and the other two children were dying.

Dr. Vann Hay, who together with his patients had been thrown out of his Phnom Penh clinic on April 17, also started northward on Highway 5 and in all spent a month in villages and on various roads and trails. Of all the agonies composing the spectacle of horror he witnessed, the most difficult for him to bear was the ordeal of the children.

"We must have passed the body of a child every two hundred meters. Most of them died of gastrointestinal afflictions which caused complete dehydration. Not only were they undernourished, but hygiene conditions were terrible. Also, the days were extremely hot, while it often rained at night. Since we had to walk all day, there was no time to build any shelter for these children. They were exposed to heat and rain mercilessly. I had some medication with me, but most children brought to me were beyond help, considering the conditions. They would have required massive dosages of medication and lengthy rest afterward. Neither was available. Thus, I decided to save my pills for those children who could survive despite the long march. It was an awful decision to take. I could see no other solution."

Comparable conditions prevailed on the other national highways out of Phnom Penh, as well as on the main routes leading out of the other evacuated cities. Pin-Sam Phon, the Catholic Relief Service worker, was in the border city of Poipet on April 24, when the communists suddenly evicted the entire population and marched the people southeastward.

"There were thousands of us on the road, and all of us were frightened. It was around eleven A.M. and very hot already. People had assembled some belongings hastily. Some had wrapped them up, carrying parcels; others pulled little handcarts behind them; others had thrown everything they could into enormous soup pots on wheels, which they pushed before them.* The road is choked with people; you couldn't find a square inch of empty space, and we advance very slowly only under the burning sun. Some people stop by the road to cook a little rice and rest. But there is no water. We have to take it from the gutter—stale rainwater—ditches where cattle usually drink from. In normal times we wouldn't even wash our feet in this dirty, muddy liquid. At a distance of a few kilometers the road becomes very bad, and people have to leave behind their carts and soup pots with their belongings. Many of them cry. The Khmer Rouge who accompanied us weren't even looking at us. At no time did they tell us where we were going, let alone ask if we needed anything. . . .

"On April 26 by four A.M. the road was again full of people continuing their flight to nowhere. Around Kop Toueh I saw about twenty corpses of old people and children—by the roadside, under trees and in the fields. They had not died a violent death; they had died from the wind sickness.† I also saw some corpses of newborn babies. They belonged to women who had given birth by the roadside."

Chorn Dayouth, a twenty-five-year-old gemstone

*The pots were used by merchants who sold "Chinese soup" from door to door and in the markets.

†Wind sickness is a term employed in the Cambodian countryside to explain a death whose cause is not apparent. It means that a "wind spirit" or "evil spirit" entered the body and stole life away.

grader, was locked in a solid phalanx of about 40,000 people expelled from Pailin and herded northward into the jungles. "Walking for two days, we covered about twenty kilometers. Along the road I saw many bodies, mainly old people who had obviously died of exhaustion. Women were giving birth by the roadside and had to get up and walk on immediately afterward. Often they had no milk, and the Khmer Rouge had nothing to give the babies. I don't think they could survive. I also saw some bodies without heads and bodies eaten on by animals or crows."

Son Phan, an eighteen-year-old high-school student, saw much the same while passing through the village of Prek Phnov, about 9 kilometers northwest of Phnom Penh. "There were many deaths. I saw one woman die while giving birth to a baby in the street. Children died of starvation or from diarrhea because health conditions were terrible. There were no medicines available, and the Khmer Rouge were not helping people at all."

Because the communist troops enforcing the exodus were so few in number compared to the multitudes being herded into the countryside, they could not space themselves along every kilometer of the many lines of march. During unguarded interludes people sometimes could rest or stray off onto unwatched side roads or trails to wander about on their own until they encountered a roving patrol or were corralled by *Angka* officials at a checkpoint or village. Occasionally exiles inadvertently were accorded opportunity to rest because of indecision by their overseers. Thousands of Battambang residents being marched southward were stopped at a highway barricade and told, "*Angka* has given orders to keep you here until *Angka* gives out new orders." In an effort to thin out the masses, troops at times compelled tens of thousands to wait while forcing a few thousand to proceed.

Generally, on the main highways, however, the march was well guarded by troops stationed at checkpoints every few kilometers and by squads accompanying the migrants at intervals of every 200 or 300 meters. Wherever troops were present, they usually demanded that the people walk throughout the day at as brisk a pace as the congestion allowed. The weary who pleaded exhaustion and begged for rest were greeted with jeers and threats.

When people in a column straggling west on Highway 4 complained of heat and thirst, a soldier grinned and said, "We have withstood hardship during five years and one month. Why can't you resist just for a few days?"

A group of families, including numerous small children, sat down by the highway outside Battambang, having walked much of the day. A soldier who discovered them shouted, "We have walked for hundreds of kilometers to fight the war, and we were never tired. You walk for a few kilometers only, and already you are unable to go on. If you cannot do any better than that, the best thing would be if we killed all of you."

And in fact, laggards often were killed. Dr. Vann Hay during the first days of his trek northward from the capital saw soldiers cut down five or six people who persistently failed to keep pace. "They would give a first warning, then a second warning; then they would shoot. Most of the ones I saw being killed were elderly."

Many executions of stragglers occurred out of sight but within earshot of the marchers. "The communists would take them into a field; then we would hear three or four rifle shots," recalls librarian Ea Than. "The soldiers would reappear alone."

Lawyer Ho Mey, who was one of the hundreds of thousands walking northward on Highway 5, states: "The population was tired. They stopped to rest. As they rested, the Khmer Rouge told them to proceed. If we went slow or didn't listen to them, whoever did not move to proceed, they pulled them by the arm and shot them. And rest was not allowed for long. That is, after you cook rice to eat, you must proceed. If you don't proceed, you are shot."

Indeed, throughout the Emigration all over the land, the discipline imposed by *Angka Loeu* was so draconian that people were frequently executed summarily for any hint of disobedience or protest. On Highway 5 near Prek Kdam, Ho Mey stood in line waiting to receive his cup of rice from a truck. A few steps ahead of him a man of about thirty-five argued that the ration he had just been given was insufficient for his family. "We have three growing children," he pleaded. "Couldn't I please have a second tinful?" As the man's horrified wife and children watched, soldiers grabbed each of the man's arms, dragged him some ten meters out of the line and riddled him with three bursts from Chinese submachine guns. Ho Mey remembers how the man's wife collapsed, screaming and pounding the ground. "He was given no warning. I suppose it was meant to intimidate us."

A few days later, as rice was being doled out from the back of a truck farther down the highway, the communist escort singled out a boy who looked about thirteen, led him into the field and shot him.

Returning to the refugee lines, one of the executioners said to the fearfully silent witnesses, "This boy was a cheat. He tried to get a second helping. We don't like cheats. There is no room for them in our country."

Troops manning a barricade on National Highway 4 about 25 kilometers west of Phnom Penh around noon on April 20 halted a congregation of several hundred exiles and diverted them onto a dirt road. "Walk along, and you will come to the pagoda of Ta Phem," a soldier told them. "*Angka* will help you there." Joining hundreds of other refugees already at the pagoda little more than a kilometer off the highway, the newcomers asked a soldier for the promised "help" from *Angka Loeu*, but he knew nothing about it, and they decided to cook a meal with their own rice. The pagoda well was dry, and the only available water lay in a dark, odorous pond on which floated the bloated bodies of two government soldiers. Looking for wood so they could boil the befouled water, some of the new arrivals stumbled upon the body of another soldier, his hands bound behind his back. About 3 P.M. a communist officer announced through a megaphone, "You cannot stay here. Move on immediately. This area is not safe yet. We have to clean it up first."

It was too much for a young man whom, on the basis of his speech and appearance, the others thought to be an intellectual. "So why did you make us come here if the area is not safe yet and if we have to move again?" he shouted.

A few seconds later the young man was dead. The equally young communist officer, who had whipped out a pistol and shot him, shouted, "In times of revolution, protest is forbidden."

Outcasts from Poipet, diverted off the main highway toward the jungle, reached the tiny village of Rong Kor and asked for water. A villager pointed them to a well, but thirsty as they were, they suddenly stopped drinking. Soldiers were prodding a man in his mid-thirties through the village, alternately commanding, "Go quickly," and "Stop!" Meanwhile, they vilified him with the filthiest deprecations. Then they killed him suddenly, ripping open the back of his body with bursts from Chinese AK-47 machine guns.

One witness to the execution was twenty-three-year-old Kuy Hong Taing, who had become a policeman, then been discharged because of partially disabling wounds suffered when he tried to arrest a cattle thief. Kuy asked a villager why the man had been killed. "I was told the man had come from the neighboring village to trade some clothes for rice because his seven children were hungry. The Khmer Rouge caught him and told him this was an act of sabotage because he was spreading news that there was a food shortage. And people did not have the right to leave one village for another to barter."

The killing during the great exodus was all the more terrifying because so much of it was unpredictable and pointless. A former truck driver, Thiounn Kamel, was swept up in the throngs pushed out of Phnom Penh on National Highway 1. "When I couldn't move because of the crowd, I stopped on the side of the road. That time there was a truck loaded with armed Khmer Rouge. When their truck also couldn't move, they just shot at the people to clear the way and killed some of them. It was savage."

Evacuees from Kampot, the capital of southernmost Kampot Province, were marched eastward toward

Kompong Trach. On the road at a point marked
Kilometer 12 they saw a government soldier's widow
from the nearby town of Veal Renh walking with her
four young children—two sons and two daughters. A
soldier approached her and asked, "Do you have
enough food? Can you take care of all these children?"

The mother admitted that she did not and could
not.

"Then you look after the two boys," replied the
soldier. "I'll take care of your daughters for you."

He took the younger girl, a one-month-old baby, in
one arm and with his free hand led away the other, a
three-year-old. Acquaintances of the mother following a hundred or so meters behind saw the atrocity
that ensued. As soon as the mother was out of sight,
the soldier hurled both children in turn against the
trunk of a large tree, battering each to death. If his
purpose was to terrify onlookers, he succeeded.

Hungry, thirsty, exhausted, dirty and terrorized,
often ill or grief-stricken, worried about fretting, crying children whom they could not comfort, benumbed by what had happened and fearful of what
might happen next, the wretched threw away, one by
one, belongings whose weight they no longer could
bear. Deluded into believing they would be away only
briefly, some people tried to haul with them for
safekeeping possessions which were useless in the
countryside but prized because they were family treasures or had been earned through extreme effort. Such
articles—television sets, small refrigerators, air con-
ditioners, sewing machines, pieces of furniture—
were among the first to be discarded. Dropped next
were mattresses, blankets, clothes, stoves, crockery,

pots, pans, toys. Cambodian money being worthless, gold, jewelry, precious stones and U.S. dollars became the only currency coveted or accepted. Any article now was valued primarily according to how much it might contribute to survival.

The possessions of the people dwindled further at marshaling centers established in pagodas and village markets, as well as at highway checkpoints, where soldiers stripped bypassers of any "luxury" items they had failed to hide. The proscribed list of goods included radios, fountain pens, ball-point pens, pencils, identification papers, watches, jewelry, cigarette lighters, clothing reflecting foreign fashions and all medicine. The soldiers also grabbed canned milk, often the only nourishment families had for their babies, and sometimes they even took away eyeglasses.

Early in the march some people abandoned their automobiles, perhaps because they lacked the strength to push them interminably, perhaps because in the congestion their retention seemed futile. A majority of owners, though, tried to keep vehicles for what they felt were practical reasons. Even though it had to be pushed, a car provided a measure of comfort and shelter for relatives unable to walk, the means of transporting belongings and the prospective means of returning home when return was allowed, as most initially believed it would be.

But at a radius of about 20 kilometers outside Phnom Penh troops began sporadically commandeering vehicles. Some tried to be polite and reassuring. "Angka Loeu will forward your car to your new address," one said to a man who could only stare and marvel that anyone should be expected to believe such a statement. Other soldiers were more blunt. "The use of cars and motorcycles is forbidden from now on," announced one. "Your car is taken by *Angka*. You have no longer any right to own a car," said another.

Refugees stopped for the night on Highway 4 heard rifle shots, then an announcement over a loud-speaker: "*Angka* is asking you for your cars and motorcycles. You must leave them here."

People jumped up in consternation and anger. "This cannot be done!" ... "What will we do?" ... "We have old parents and small children who cannot walk great distances!" ... "How can we continue without our cars?"

Prach Chhea, a twenty-three-year-old law student, saw a man in his sixties with a bald patch, who looked like a civil servant, get up and walk over to a communist soldier. "Your order won't work," he said. "Let us first go to wherever you want us to go. Once we have reached our destination, we'll turn over our cars. But how can we reach our destination without a car?"

"Now is the time of revolution! And you don't talk back to *Angka!*" the soldier shouted in reply. Then he sprayed the man with bursts of machine-gun bullets. The man immediately crumpled to the ground, and several others around him also fell.

Later that night as women wept at the prospect of having to proceed by foot without the supplies borne by their cars, a young communist soldier, actually a boy, was moved to comfort them. "Don't worry," he said earnestly. "Farther on there is *Angka*, and *Angka* will help you."

Because of general confusion, laxity at checkpoints

or the comparative weakness of controls on back roads in the early days of the Emigration, some people managed to keep automobiles a while longer. But before too long all were seized by *Angka Loeu.* Most were pushed into fields and abandoned, overturned or vandalized, with their tires slashed, windows cracked and doors left hanging open. The wrecked cars, the vast litter of discarded belongings, the empty hospital beds, the stark trees stripped of all edible leaves and bark, the ever-present corpses, some decapitated, some dismembered, all rotting and exuding stomach-turning stench made stretches of the countryside look like a malign, surrealistic junkyard.

With the confiscation of vehicles, soldiers dropped pretenses and began to tell the people a truth: "From now on, everybody will work in the rice paddies." No attempt was made to explain or justify the deceit perpetrated in the cities when the populations were told that they would be away for "a day or two" or "a few days" or "a period of time." Now the people understood they had been betrayed. And realization that all they had was irretrievably lost, that their lives were irreversibly changed, produced trauma among many.

Parted families, whose sole consolation had been the prospect of reunion at home once the evacuation ended, now panicked into frantic, futile searches for one another. A physician, still attired in the white smock and surgeon's cap he was wearing when rousted out of the operating room at Preah Ket Melea Hospital in Phnom Penh, desperately hunted along Highway 5 for his eighty-two-year-old mother. He risked his life by darting backward and forward in and out of crowds rather than continuing to march ahead, and friends told him it was impossible to find anyone among the hundreds of thousands on the highway. Yet the psychological effects of the *Angka Loeu* revelation of the future were such that this rational, intelligent man, experienced in coping with emergency, persisted in the irrational and hopeless search.

Others chose death rather than the life they now foresaw, and suicides were reported on virtually all the main highways. Art student Norodom Vorapongs saw about a dozen people, men, women and children, drown themselves in ponds around the village of Koki. Other refugees saw a middle-aged couple embrace, then jump into the Mekong and disappear beneath the water in each other's arms. About 20 kilometers northwest of Phnom Penh, where Highway 5 runs quite close to the Mekong, fifteen people, thought by witnesses to be members of a Chinese merchant's family, roped themselves together. Solemnly they moved to the banks of the river and plunged into the waters in a mass suicide. Another Phnom Penh merchant succeeded through all the searches in concealing a great sum of Cambodian currency. Upon learning that all money had been abolished, he hanged himself in a hut at the village of Leuk Dek. The next day an *Angka* official convened refugees stopped in the village and said of the dead man, "People like him should all kill themselves, for we don't need them."

The loss of vehicles, accumulated fatigue and the *Angka Loeu* practice of killing those who faltered increasingly combined to confront families with a heart-rending choice. When a relative could not walk or keep pace, then he or she had to be carried. When the rest of the family became so weakened that they could not carry the disabled, then they had to decide whether to leave the loved one behind or lag together and risk the death of all.

Among tens of thousands of families marching south on National Highway 4 was a slender, pretty Khmer Airlines stewardess named Lon. She and her husband took turns carrying their four-month-old daughter Vathana. The infant was accustomed to canned milk and baby food because Lon, needing to return to work as soon as possible after childbirth, had not breast-fed her. Now the canned food the couple brought with them from Phnom Penh was gone, and the mother's body was incapable of producing milk. Herself suffering the effects of malnutrition and dehydration, Lon felt fainter and fainter in the searing heat. But hoping somewhere, some way, to find sustenance for the baby, she struggled to match the pace required by soldiers who periodically yelled, "Move on! Move on!"

Finally, though, she knew she was going to collapse, and in tears, she begged her husband to forsake her, to try to save their daughter and himself. The husband hesitated, then reached for the baby. As he cradled her in his arms, the infant smiled and laughed at him. He turned back and through his own tears said to his wife, "We stay together."

Friends who observed this scene and who themselves had to move on quickly understood, as probably did the husband, that he really was saying, "We die together."

Others decided differently. Generally, they gently laid the grandparent or child, the husband or wife, the father or mother, the brother or sister by the roadside and walked away in grief and guilt. Major Pech Kim Eng, who was on the march out of Phnom Penh, sums up the process that was repeated myriad times all over Cambodia thus: "I have seen them abandon one old person. They carried that person, but there was no hope. They took the person to a comfortable place and went farther. That family was afraid to carry farther. The weight was unbearable, and they knew the person could not live, and, as the Khmer Rouge ordered them to move at gunpoint, they had no choice."

The chaotic upheaval increased in magnitude as the communists began emptying villages located in territory controlled by the government at the end of the war. Now peasants, along with urban residents, suddenly were jerked from their homes of a lifetime and thrown into the milling masses of exiles. The *Angka Loeu* determination to overturn the lives of everybody was so extreme that some fishermen were turned into farmers and farmers into fishermen.

Like her parents and grandparents before them, Mom Hol, a forty-five-year-old mother of ten, had lived all her life on the little fishing island of Kaphi off the Cambodian coast in the Gulf of Thailand. One morning communist troops landed, rounded up Mom, her children and the 100-odd families inhabiting the island, sailed them to the mainland and drove them into the jungle. They kept behind a few fishermen to train soldiers imported to take over the island and fish.

Constant uncertainty and fear about the future accompanied and compounded all the agonies of the march. People could not be sure of where they finally were going or what awaited them when they arrived. Thousands of Pailin residents were driven northward along a narrow, jammed dirt road pocked with holes. After they had walked half a day, they were halted by soldiers, who ordered them to turn around and march back in the direction whence they came. The next day soldiers ordered them north again, and at nightfall of the second day they reached the village of Sala Krau, from which the communists also had expelled everybody. Their escort forbade them to enter the village, and so they had to sleep on the ground outside. The third morning the soldiers commanded a portion of the crowd to proceed eastward into the jungle. Among them was the young gemstone grader Chorn Dayouth.

"After two days we had covered about twenty kilometers, and the Khmer Rouge made us stop in the jungle in an area called Sre Anteak [which means the Field of Animal Traps in English]. There were about two thousand of us, and we were told to build huts for ourselves. First we built just a little roof to protect ourselves from the rain; then we went about collecting bamboo and straw for real huts. It took us two weeks to build a hut, for we had no tools for cutting down bamboo, no saws, no nails or hammer. We used a small kitchen knife to cut lianas, which we then used to tie together the bamboo. None of us had ever done this kind of work before, and we were not very good at it."

Among the 2,000 attempting to carve a settlement out of the "Field of Animal Traps" were a number of intellectuals and university students. One day Chorn politely and curiously asked a communist guard, "Aren't you going to use all these educated people to help you run the country?"

"No!" the soldier replied flatly. "Everybody is the same. Everybody has to work in the rice paddy."

"But look, we have no rice paddies here, or rice, or medication of any kind," Chorn said. "How are you going to make two thousand people live under such conditions?"

"We have fought a war for five years," the soldier responded. "Do you think we had all those things then?"

Angka Loeu distributed no food at Sre Anteak, and the exiles had to depend on their own waning supplies or whatever they could find in the jungle. When their huts were at last finished, they asked where were the rice paddies they were supposed to cultivate. That evening the soldiers called them together and announced that since *Angka Loeu* had no food to give them, they must move on to another area where there were rice paddies. Their arduous labors of two weeks going for naught, the migrants in the morning resumed the march, fighting their way farther into the jungle in the direction the soldiers vaguely had pointed.

As the millions advanced farther from the cities and dispersed over wider areas, soldiers or *Angka Loeu* commissars at checkpoints increasingly told people that they should return to their native villages. Some had been given such instructions in Phnom Penh, and some did succeed in finding their way back to their birthplaces. However, the approximately 1,500,000 urban residents who had been born and reared in the cities had no native villages. Myriad others had no place to go because their native villages had been destroyed in the war or evacuated by the communists afterward. And many families in the pell-mell exodus had been forced along routes that took them far away from their native villages.

Angka Loeu, by taking away identification papers, enabled people to assume new identities and claim any village they wished as their place of origin. In quest of some place less harsh than the one they had just seen, countless people wandered on as long as strength allowed, telling interrogating patrols that they were bound for their "native village."

However, sooner or later, at some barricade or village, the exiles encountered an *Angka* commander who paid no heed to any explanation or plea, and there the exodus ended. As if casting a net into a sea of fish, the commander arbitrarily would haul the people off the road and order his troops to march them to a new settlement selected for them by caprice.

The experience of the young school teacher Yen Savannary was typical. Together with his younger brother, a medical student, and a group of friends, he wandered for a month until May 18, when they were halted in the village of Chhnok Trou west of Kompong Chhnang. Communist soldiers, including twelve-year-old girls, forced them at gunpoint on a three-day trek into the jungle, periodically firing in the air to frighten them onward. As the jungle became denser and darker, Yen became more afraid. The thought that if the soldiers elected to kill him now, no one would ever know or care recurred. Early on the third day they arrived at a new village called An-chhang Roung, consisting of freshly built huts and about 500 migrants. Nowhere around were there fields or rice paddies or water. The village chief greeted his new wards: "Don't try to escape. You will be shot on sight. Now, you have three days to build huts for yourselves. On the fourth day you will begin clearing the forest."

By early June the Emigration was over. Some 3,500,000 people from the cities and probably another 500,000 from villages in territory controlled by the government on April 17 had been uprooted and scattered throughout the land. The highways out of Phnom Penh were barren and quiet. The corpses were deteriorating into skeletons; the hospital beds, cars, sewing machines were rusting.

Dr. Vann Hay had escaped to Vietnam, and he looked back over the route he had followed—from Phnom Penh northwest toward Oudong, then south again along the Mekong and southeast on Highway 1 to the South Vietnamese border. "I was thinking about all the bodies I had seen during one month, plus all the sick people who came to see me, half of whom I knew were not going to live. I used to see between twenty and thirty sick people every day. Extrapolating to cover the area which I had traversed, between Oudong and the border, plus the estimated number of inhabitants at the time, I figured that between twenty thousand and thirty thousand people must have died just during the first month, just in the one area described."

For those who lived, the worst was yet to come.

VI

LIFE AND DEATH IN
THE NEW VILLAGES

Ngy Duch was a tall, lean, muscular youth of twenty-two with a narrow face, dark eyes and straight black hair. Buddhism had taught him never to inflict pain on another human being and to abhor the war that caused so much grief to his countrymen. When news of peace reached the town of Pailin, he had celebrated thankfully, playing his bamboo flute late into the night.

However, despite his gentleness toward others, Ngy was better equipped than most to cope with harsh circumstances. As a teenager he had left the home of his parents, who were poor farmers in central Cambodia, and had become a gem prospector, a grueling pursuit demanding fortitude and perseverance. Venturing into almost inaccessible jungle climes where few others quested, digging from the first to the last light of day, he had eventually struck a rich vein of sapphires. Suddenly prosperous, he had brought his mother, six younger brothers and sisters and three cousins to Pailin and had moved them into a comfortable house by a pagoda. His sixty-year-old mother suffered from multiple ailments, including a severe heart condition, and physicians were not always quickly available. So Ngy had learned the rudiments of coronary care and bought a stethoscope, syringes and medicine with which to minister to her in an emergency.

Realizing that the communists actually intended to drive everyone out of Pailin, Ngy hastily removed the wheels from motorcycles he had given the family and, together with boards, built three pushcarts. He padded one as best he could for his mother and loaded the others with all the medicine, food, clothing, blankets and other necessities immediately available. He also took along gold, jewels and his bamboo flute.

For twenty-three days Ngy shepherded his relatives eastward through the jungle toward their native area of Kompong Thom. Pounding rains darkened the days and turned trails into quagmires. The carts sometimes broke apart in the mud, but each time Ngy repaired and reinforced them with branches. At night he lit fires to dry and warm the family and reminded all of happier times by playing nostalgic Khmer folk songs on the flute. Twice the family rested in new refugee settlements, and in each Ngy persuaded the *Angka* chieftain to allow them to continue onward toward their native village.

The family in late May stopped at a third village, Ampil Pram Daum, intending only to spend the night. However, an *Angka* boss, a Comrade Mon, declared that continuation of their journey was "out of the question." The village needed laborers, and the family would stay and work. Explaining that all property now was community property, Mon's lieutenants confiscated the family's remaining supplies, except for the gold and jewels, which his mother buried beneath the hut, and some pills Ngy hid in a bamboo pole for his mother. He was allowed to keep his flute on the strict condition that he play only revolutionary songs.

Ampil Pram Daum, located about 70 kilometers northwest of Battambang, once was a large village in the midst of fertile rice fields. The original residents had disappeared, and their vacant houses, though damaged and decaying, could have provided adequate shelter for many of the approximately 2,000 refugees *Angka Loeu* had consigned to the locale. However, consistent with its determination to wipe away the past entirely and start society anew, *Angka Loeu* prohibited anyone from living in the old village. All had to build their own huts on the edge of the forest and create a completely New Village.

What Ngy experienced in Ampil Pram Daum was typical of what millions of other Cambodians experienced. Sooner or later *Angka Loeu* drove virtually everybody from the cities into one of thousands of New Villages, such as Ampil Pram Daum, that were being hewn out of the wilderness. While conditions in these settlements varied according to the availability of water and the fertility of land, the regimen of work, life and death dictated by *Angka Loeu* was largely uniform throughout the countryside.

Characteristically, a New Village at birth consisted of little except a designated area of land, the people shanghaied to develop it and *Angka* supervisors. *Angka* allotted each arriving family a space, usually about 5 meters square, on which to build a hut. Normally, neither materials nor tools were provided, so the family had to forage for bamboo, branches, palm leaves, straw, grass or whatever else useful the forest and jungles might yield. The average hut had no walls and thus was vulnerable to wind-driven rains and curious glances. Ngy was able to build a hut for his family and another for his cousins in about two weeks.

Upon completion of the hut family members joined the common labor force engaged in clearing trees and underbrush, plowing for the planting of rice and erection of irrigation dikes. Children under six, women in the last stages of pregnancy, the very aged and, generally but not always, the extremely ill were exempted from work. Otherwise, having been awakened by a gong, everybody labored from 5:30 or 6 A.M. to 11 A.M. and 1 or 2 to 5 P.M. seven days a week, irrespective of rain or heat. In some settlements work resumed for three hours at night if the moon was out. Men, women and children were segregated into separate work parties and kept apart in the fields. Except during the midday break, Angka guards allowed neither rest nor conversation during work.

For urban dwellers unaccustomed to hard labor, weakened by rigors of the march and ignorant of agriculture, the physical demands were excruciating. Widespread insufficiency of oxen or water buffalo and even rudimentary tools such as plows, axes, hoes and shovels made them even more painful. Men had to pull plows themselves and, when plows were lacking, till the soil with bamboo poles. Both men and women frequently had to dig dirt for dikes with their bare hands. And they tried to fell trees with ropes or crude axes fashioned from sticks and stones.

Although Ngy convinced Comrade Mon that his mother was too ill and weak to work, the rest of the family labored nine to ten hours a day. Ngy was assigned to a group of 215 people, and for a month he pulled a plow as if he were an ox. Later he helped build dikes, scooping up and packing dirt with his hands, which he often bruised and scraped.

In the evenings, unless field work was required under the moonlight, *Angka Loeu* compelled all New Villagers throughout Cambodia to attend ideological lectures that droned on for three or four hours. These customarily were delivered in communal huts by itinerant *Angka Loeu* commissars, village chieftains or members of the appointed committee that administered each settlement.* Frequently, the assembled also witnessed one of the gravest of village events, a ceremony known as a *kosang*, the Khmer word for "construction." A *kosang* was a formal and ritualistic warning to someone who had displeased *Angka Loeu*. The transgressor was expected to submit to public

---

*In time *Angka Loeu* imposed a rigid hierarchical organization on the new settlements. The French scholar François Ponchaud, on the basis of interviews with numerous refugees, describes the organization thus: ". . . the entire population has been organized like an army in time of war. Every village is composed of groups of ten families, called *krom*, with the group chiefs appointed by *Angka*. These *krom* form villages, *phum*, with a village chief and several 'presidents.' These presidents preside over specific groups—the young people, the girls, the old people, the children—and all are appointed by *Angka*. Several villages together form a canton, *khum*, the seat of the 'cadres,' *kamaphibal*, who are members of the army. They not only direct all the work, but they have the power to decide over life and death of the population."

Refugees interviewed by the authors additionally said that

humiliation, then to "construct" himself or herself into a good and pure person by confessing and repenting the sin alleged. Always a *kosang* evoked silence and fear among the onlookers, for everyone quickly learned that no one ever received more than two *kosangs*.

About the middle of June, while working in the forest, Ngy stepped on a sharp piece of bamboo which penetrated almost all the way through his foot. His whole leg swelled, he developed a high fever and pains shot up to his waist, so he hobbled to Comrade Mon and requested a few days' respite from work to recuperate. "Such a tiny wound is not enough of a reason for staying home," Comrade Mon said impassively.

That night Ngy received his first *kosang*, as committee members took turns berating him: "You must learn to live with pain. You must not be soft and give up at the slightest little bit of pain. You must not be lazy, trying to get out of your share of work whenever you have a chance." There followed a litany: Ngy was free. Ngy was equal. Ngy was happy. Humbly, Ngy admitted that he had been a lazy malingerer and

---

under a village chieftain are several appointed "chairmen" or "presidents" responsible for designated functions such as education, logistics or spying on the villagers. According to some, *Angka* in selecting village functionaries seemed to give preference to illiterates or the least educated.

At the end of the war, *Angka Loeu* commanded a military force estimated to number no more than between 60,000 and 70,000 combat troops—a ratio of approximately 1 communist soldier to every 100 Cambodians. Many refugees reported that in their settlements only a few soldiers were permanently present. The elaborate organization of the new settlements may help explain why so few have been able to enforce their will on so many.

pledged to shirk no more, to work honorably for *Angka Loeu*.

Kosangs were followed by Revolutionary Education, during which speakers by rote repeated claims, admonitions and slogans with evangelical fervor. "You must forget everything you have learned.... You must learn to hate the former regime and the American imperialists.... You must work hard to produce much.... We are building the only true communism.... Our communism will be better than in Russia or China, where there are still classes.... You are now free.... You are happy.... Give up all your material possessions, for they now belong to *Angka*. Give up your selfishness.... Cast out your vice, all the capital sins.... Accept giving your whole life to *Angka* ... Be prepared to sacrifice yourself.... Your respect for *Angka* must be absolute and complete.... Even the slightest infraction can lead to disappearance...."

Depicting the consequences of offending *Angka Loeu*, its missionaries habitually warned that the Wheel of History would grind down anyone who disobeyed or flagged. Endlessly repeated, the references to the mystical Wheel of History conjured up terrifying images. A student who underwent prolonged indoctrination recalls: "The words induced us to think of a huge roller with unimaginable weight, behind us all the time and ready to crush any one of us into powder should we happen to trip or slow down for any reason." Still another frightening specter was raised by the oft-given warning: "If you are lazy, we will send you to *Angka Loeu* to reconstitute your brains."

The necessity to subordinate all life to toil in the

fields and to suffuse all thoughts with hatred of things foreign, particularly American, formed other dominant themes of the ideological indoctrination. The wearing of Western clothes or hairstyles, the possession of foreign goods and even the utterance of a foreign word were proclaimed punishable offenses. Frequently the commissars required villagers to memorize and chant slogans conveying the new orthodoxy. Some were: "I must put my whole mind on my work. My mind belongs to *Angka*. . . . I may not wear any color but black. . . . I must forget about the former regime. . . . A father has no right to spank his child. . . . I must not drink alcohol or gamble. . . . I must not play around with women. . . ."

The strictures against sex were especially severe. An *Angka Loeu* commissar summoned exiles temporarily staying in the village of Leuk Dek to a special meeting solely to discuss sex in the new Cambodia. "We do not want girls and boys to be together. Everybody should concentrate exclusively on work. Therefore, we have separated by sexes. Sexual relations among unmarried couples are strictly forbidden. . . . We do not have any sexual problems. A Red Khmer boy can spend the night under the same mosquito net with a Red Khmer girl, and no sexual relations will take place."* The commissar concluded by announc-

---

*Dr. Vann Hay, the physician routed from his Phnom Penh clinic along with wounded patients, heard this lecture and later commented: "I wasn't particularly amazed at the moral strength of the Red Khmer boys versus the Red Khmer girls. The latter were unbelievably dirty. Their clothes were shapeless and filthy; their hair was cut in the most unbecoming style. Sexual attraction starts in the eye of the beholder. Certainly, no one would risk capital punishment for a fling with a Red Khmer girl."

ing that henceforth boys and girls caught holding hands would be executed.

The village chieftain of Kompong Ley, a Comrade Seng, often inveighed against the evils of extramarital sex and warned, "If we discover such an affair, the people concerned will be killed."

Phal So Vichet, who served in the postwar communist army and observed life in several New Villages, states: "Love was strictly forbidden. Not only secret meetings between a boy and a girl prompted a warning, but even the use of the word *oun*, which means darling. The Red Khmers kept saying, "Don't behave like the French or the Japanese, who have illicit love affairs.' Five young people, three boys and two girls, disregarded even their second warning and were finally executed. I saw their bodies at some distance from our work site."

Pa Sothy, a math student who slipped through four New Villages en route to Thailand, says, "Girls and boys had to stay apart because love was forbidden. There was no love anywhere; only hard work."

While making extramarital sex punishable by death, *Angka Loeu* also sought to inhibit love within the family and to break up traditional family relationships. Parents were stripped of the right to discipline children. They might "request" a given action or form of behavior, but children were free to disregard the "request." And children were singled out for the most intensive brainwashing, calculated to estrange them further from their parents and transfer their loyalty from family to *Angka Loeu*. In the village of Khna Sar university student Ung Sok Choeu observed: "The only subjects the children were being taught were revolutionary thinking and the aims of the Khmer

Rouge struggle and how to detect the enemies of both. As a result, all the children turned into little Khmer Rouge spies, reporting everything that was said at home." Another university student, Prach Chhea, saw similar effects in the New Village of Thnal Bat. "There was no school at Thnal Bat. The children worked like everybody else. One day the Khmer Rouge came to recruit young people for their army. In each village they picked one girl and one boy. In our village they both were illiterate. Four days later they were back, spouting Khmer Rouge propaganda. I never knew illiterates would learn so quickly. They kept telling us we should do as *Angka* told us; otherwise, we would be done away with."

In Ampil Pram Daum the conversion of children into fanatic, venomous spies was especially successful. Their reports led to numerous *kosangs,* and some derived a heady sense of power from the knowledge that they could place the life of any elder in jeopardy. In time the mere sight of them made Ngy afraid. Awareness that their own children might report their words precluded parents from speaking freely to them or to each other if the children were within earshot. Husbands and wives were further restrained from communicating frankly with each other or expressing any differences that might lead to a quarrel because *Angka Loeu* either separated or executed couples caught arguing more than twice. Beyond all this the routine of work and nocturnal indoctrination, coupled with segregation in the fields, left families with little time to be together. And the discretionary time they did have usually had to be spent in search of food, for terrible hunger soon stalked the New Villages.

During the first six to eight weeks after evacuation
of the cities *Angka Loeu* generally succeeded in dis-
tributing a ration of one condensed-milk can full of
rice—or about 250 grams—daily to each person (in
some settlements, small children and others who did
not work received half this amount). Additionally,
small amounts of salt were dispensed irregularly.
Much of the rice initially delivered to the New Villages
came from the large stocks supplied by the Americans
and captured by the communists in Phnom Penh. As
these stocks dwindled, so did the already inadequate
rations, and by midsummer many villagers were receiving only half a milk can of rice, which provided
fewer than 400 calories. Because this caloric intake
was insufficient to sustain life, survival depended on
success in extracting additional sustenance from the
forests and jungles. As villagers depleted their sur-
roundings of fish, field crabs, snails, wild fruit and
berries, they looked to birds and animals to teach
them what they might safely consume. "We ate whatever we saw the oxen eat, figuring it couldn't harm
us," recalls Ung Beng Chun, a gem digger who lived
for six months in the New Villages of northwest Cambodia. "Our main diet was a very bitter fruit, which
we had to soak in water before we could eat it. We also
ate the bark of a tree. We'd first scrape it, then boil it
in water until it turned into a thick paste." Soon des-
peration drove the exiles to eat literally anything
edible—algae, leaves, tree bark, bindweed, locusts,
grasshoppers, lizards, snakes, rats, worms, termites.

In the hundreds of New Villages around Mount
Tippadei people devoured inedible grass and vines.
Their skin turned yellow, and they vomited blood,
and their bodies so shriveled that the outline of their

bones was visible. Elsewhere malnutrition, particularly lack of salt, caused disabling swelling of the legs. Anemic children were infested with sores, and their physiological reserves were so exhausted that the smallest scratches failed to heal.

The food shortage reached famine proportions in late August and early September, when rice deliveries to large areas of northwest Cambodia ceased altogether. The last rice arrived in the New Village of Beng Katom, 30 kilometers north of Pailin, on September 10. The communist commander of the village, a Comrade Dui, evidently was personally compassionate. He assembled the villagers, sadly told them there would be no more rice and authorized them to forage on their own in a radius of up to 3 kilometers from the settlement. But many were now so enfeebled that they barely could walk, and two men who climbed a tall tamarind tree in quest of fruit lost their hold and fell to their death.

Not far away from Beng Katom there was an established communist village inhabited by a minority group of Laotian and Thai descent, and here food was still available. Comrade Dui through the wife of the Beng Katom village chairman discreetly passed the word that his people were free to barter whatever valuables they possessed for rice in the old village so long as they kept quiet about the trade. For a while some villagers who had secreted gold or jewels on their bodies survived on food obtained from the old villagers. But as Yan Nam, a stonecutter from near Battambang, remembers: "Those people without gold and jewels or those who ran out of them began dying of starvation. You could see their bleeding sores, swollen stomachs, swollen legs. Even small children must use sticks for walking. Some ate wild plants or roots that were poisonous and died."

Yan Nam asked Comrade Dui how the village could endure the famine. In despair, Comrade Dui replied, "*Angka* cannot do anything, cannot give anything. Let the old die. Just save the children."

However, in a number of villages no attempt was made to save orphaned children too young to be useful to *Angka Loeu*. Chou Try, a schoolteacher from Phum Srok, near Sisophon, states: "Many orphaned or abandoned children eat whatever they can find, such as the peels of bananas and oranges thrown away by the Khmer Rouge. While the Khmer Rouge were eating, the children would stand there and watch them, sometimes with tears in their eyes. Every day some villager would secretly give some food to these poor children. At night they slept outside the village where the executions take place. Nobody dared adopt these children, for the Khmer Rouge had strictly forbidden it."

Another schoolteacher saw similar sights in New Villages around Mount Tippadei. "Often while the soldiers were eating their meals together, small, emaciated children would approach and beg for food. The Khmer Rouge had issued strict orders not to give them any food. On more than one occasion they chased the little things away with sticks."

The debilitation induced by malnutrition made any malady or wound potentially fatal. Epidemics of malaria, cholera and typhoid spread as exiles from the cities carried germs acquired during the march into diverse sections of the country. And water fouled by the bodies of the dead and the wastes of the living continuously bred dysentery and other diseases.

The former communist soldier Phal So Vichet for a while was stationed at a new village, Tul Ampil, in Battambang Province, where some 5,000 exiles were settled. "There was not enough water for all of them. The same muddy little brook was used by all for washing and drinking water, and all kinds of diseases were spreading. Some days up to fifty people died."

Given the combination of epidemics, malnutrition, lack of hygiene and medical care, the death rate was high in the countryside, and all evidence indicates it rose steadily through 1975. Of the approximately 1,000 people inhabiting the New Village of Ta Orng, about 100 adults and the same number of children died in the month of June. The New Village of Sambok Ork contained 540 people when organized in late April. In the months of July and August two to five people died daily, according to the philosophy professor Phal Oudam, who was drafted to file biweekly reports of deaths to *Angka Loeu*. Out of roughly 800 inhabitants in Phum Svay Sar, north of Kompong Thom, about 150 died in the summer. Of 300 residents in Tha Yenh, southwest of Battambang, 40 percent were unable to walk, and 67 had died by October.

Conditions of life usually were better in areas of the countryside which the communists occupied before their final triumph. Yet the epidemics and food shortages ultimately spread into these regions. Soeur, an established village with a population of about 1,500 in western Cambodia, had long been under communist control. Yet by September the daily ration had dropped to three cans of unmilled rice per family, and between twenty and thirty people died each day of malaria and dysentery.

Ngy and the people of Ampil Pram Daum suffered

almost as fearfully. By September they had denuded the nearby jungles of crabs, snails, bamboo shoots, bindweed and all else edible. The inflated bellies of children protruded above spindly legs, and the people looked like skeletons draped with a thin, sickly cover of skin. Roughly 15 percent of Ngy's group had died, and of the original 215, now only 10 were strong enough to work. Ngy himself could walk only by using sticks as canes.

Although *Angka Loeu* initially seemed implacably indifferent to the death rate, it became sufficiently troubled to establish makeshift dispensaries in some of the outlying towns, which, like the cities, had been emptied. The schoolteacher Chou Try worked at one of two set up in the little town of Phum Srok outside Sisophon. "The population is weakened by lack of food, lack of suitable shelter, lack of hygiene. As a result, every day people die of malaria, typhoid fever, dysentery, beriberi or cholera. Many of the agonizing cry day and night for their mother and father to come and help them. The number of patients often reached four hundred to five hundred in each of the dispensaries. The overflow we had to put up in the empty houses whose owners had been chased away. Every month there were between three hundred and six hundred deaths.

"The almost naked bodies were thrown into shallow mass graves. Among the refugees, many had lost their entire families. Others had just one relative who survived. Near Stun Sre River, a New Village was established for one hundred families. Most of the men have died. When I left, only ten men were still alive."

However, comparatively few dared complain about the agonies they suffered or saw. Through spies and terror, *Angka Loeu* largely succeeded in spiritually isolating people from one another, in making everyone fearful of confiding in anyone else, in convincing each that he or she was alone and helpless against the omnipotence and omnipresence of *Angka Loeu*. And *Angka Loeu* quickly demonstrated that all the ferocious rhetoric about the consequences of nonconformity was, if anything, understated.

As a rule, *Angka Loeu* administered only two forms of punishment. One was the *kosang*, or warning; the other was execution. Methods of execution varied widely. People caught trying to escape or those who flagrantly defied an order customarily were killed on the spot without warning. Nor were warnings given former officers of the Lon Nol army or gendarmerie. After being unmasked by whatever means, they ordinarily were led into the jungle and shot. Others simply disappeared in the night and were not seen again unless villagers by chance happened upon the bodies while searching for something to eat.

But beginning in early summer of 1975, executions increasingly were conducted publicly and more ceremoniously. The condemned person learned of impending death when told, "*Angka Loeu* wants to reeducate you," or, "*Angka Loeu* has a new task for you," or, "*Angka Loeu* wants to see you." Relatives had to watch while their loved one was put to death by stabbing, bludgeoning, axing, garroting or decapitation. Women and children most commonly were killed by being knifed in the front of the throat or struck in the back of the neck with hoes. As the doomed person knelt to die, the relatives struggled to muffle their moans and wails lest the expressions of grief be construed as hostility toward the executioners.

High school student Sar Sam witnessed one of

these public executions in the New Village of Prek
Luong. At noon all the villagers were recalled from
the fields to the center of the settlement, where five
prisoners were standing, their hands tied behind their
backs. All were students between the ages of eighteen
and twenty-five, and according to what Sar was told,
they were guilty of ridiculing *Angka Loeu*. However,
a communist officer declared, "These five men are
traitors. They refused to work. Therefore, they should
not be allowed to live." Thereupon soldiers advanced
behind the youths, wrapped long narrow towels
around their necks and commenced to twist them,
slowly garroting the boys. Unmoved by the quickly
muffled screams of the boys, the soldiers proceeded
with the executions while the villagers silently trembled or wept in fear and horror.

Sometimes entire families were executed because
of the crimes of one or two members. At the New
Village of Tumnub Kandor math student Pa Sothy
watched a father, mother and their three children die.
The hands of all five were bound behind them, and
they were ordered to kneel. Soldiers then hit them
from behind with bamboo poles until their necks
broke and they died. After death had finally ended all
the screaming and wailing, Pa asked a soldier what
the family had done. He was told they had stolen rice.

To intensify and amplify the psychological effects
of executions among the people, the communists on
occasion exhibited bodies. Accountant Lymeng
Sanithvong, who lived in the New Village of Kop
Toueh, recalls: "One day the Red Khmers showed us
three bodies in the rice paddy. One was a high school
teacher, another a doctor and the third a mining engineer. The Red Khmers told us that they killed these

three men because they wanted to flee. They also told us how they had killed them: by hitting them in the back of the neck with hoes. 'That's how we kill people,' they said."

In terms of terror spread, a floating exhibition of the executed was one of the most successful. The communists built a bamboo raft with a low railing and on it strapped the bodies of seven men clad only in black underpants. Then they set the raft adrift on the Mongkol Borei River and let the current carry it downstream. To the countless people who saw it from the riverbanks, the message from *Angka Loeu* was unmistakable.

Probably expediency dictated the way in which most of the doomed were executed. But it would appear that sometimes *Angka Loeu* determined the manner of death according to the severity of the offense. Of all the eyewitness accounts of executions, some of the most credible and vivid emanate from the Buddhist monk Hem Samlaut, who lived in the New Village of Do Nauy deep in the jungles of northern Cambodia.

"At a distance of less than one kilometer from Do Nauy was a place where executions took place. People from the whole region, and a great many of those who had tried to cross the border into Thailand, were executed there. The first thing I heard when I arrived at the village was about this place of execution. The Khmer Rouge encouraged people to go and look at the bodies so they would see what awaited them should they try to escape. I couldn't believe what I heard, so I asked the Khmer Rouge to see the place, and they took me.

"There were three shallow ditches not deeper than

a meter. In the first one were about one hundred bodies; in the second, about eighty; and in the third, about thirty. The large majority were men, but there were some women and children among them. The Khmer Rouge took advantage of the situation to frighten me by acting like guides.

" 'This is a military man and his family,' they'd say. 'He was not only a traitor, but tried to escape as well. Over there is another military and his family. See what is awaiting you if you ever decide to escape.'

"I was very upset at the sight of the bodies and the Khmer Rouge behavior. They even told me that they made people dig a ditch, then lined them up and shot them so they would fall into the ditch. I felt something changed inside me. I hardened.

"When I visited the place of execution, none of the ditches was covered with earth. The villagers told me that they usually received orders to cover up the graves much later when the bodies were all swollen beyond recognition. Indeed, after I had been at Do Nauy for about ten days, I and a whole group of people were sent to cover a grave. After that there were no more mass executions. Every three or four days a work group was led to the site to bury five or six bodies. By that time the Khmer Rouge no longer shot their victims. They hit them in the back of the neck with a pickax in order not to waste a bullet. The Khmer Rouge kept telling all of us that the ones who tried to escape were all rich people and traitors to the communist cause. I believe that those executed in the forest were in fact people from elsewhere, because all the executions among the refugees took place in the village itself. The Khmer Rouge were constantly on the lookout for former military men. Those found out were killed.

"The first execution I witnessed at Do Nauy was that of Saray Savath, a colonel from Phnom Penh, who had been stationed at Sisophon. I knew him already before I came to the village, for the bonzes are invited to all religious holidays and celebrations by important citizens. Saray Savath never told the Red Khmers that he used to be a government officer, yet they found out nevertheless. Knowing that they had found out and were going to kill him, Saray Savath tried to escape. He was caught and given a first degree execution. That meant he was to die slowly over some days. First the Red Khmers cut off his nose and ears; then they cut a deep gash into his arm. Thus, as he was bleeding to death, his arms were tied behind his back and attached to a tree. The rope was long, so the colonel could dance around the tree with pain, and the spectators were getting a better show. For two days and two nights the colonel cried for help by his tree, but nobody was allowed to go near him. On the third day he died.

"The second execution was also a military: Captain Chheng Mom from Phnom Penh. He did not try to escape; his only crime was his rank. The Khmer Rouge were more merciful toward him. They killed him quickly with a pickax, hitting him at the back of the neck.

"The third execution touched me personally. At Do Nauy my pupil and I had met another bonze, Mom Chheng Lor, from Siem Reap. We had built our huts next to each other, and together we planned to escape. We could not talk at night, for the villagers and the Khmer Rouge were constantly spying on us. But during the day at work we managed to exchange a few words sometimes. We had finally set a date for our escape, and Mom Chheng Lor went to say good-bye to

his younger brother, who was also at Do Nauy. Some
spy heard the words exchanged between the two
brothers and went to fetch the Khmer Rouge, who
arrested the bonze right away. His young brother
came running to my hut and told me the story. I went
to the chief Khmer Rouge to beg him to spare Mom
Chheng Lor. My pupil and I were answering for his
future conduct. But all the Khmer Rouge said was,
'You mind your business, and this bonze will mind
his. He is a traitor. He is against our regime. He wants
to escape. He deserves punishment.'

"The only guarantee he was willing to accept was if
the whole village was ready to answer for (to make
themselves personally and individually responsible
for) Mom Chheng Lor. The village was assembled,
and the case presented. Finally, there was a vote, and
over one hundred inhabitants were willing to answer
for the bonze. But that was not enough for the Khmer
Rouge. They ordered Mom Chheng Lor to dig a grave.
When it was about waist deep, they asked him to
stand in it. Then one of the Khmer Rouge hit him in
the neck with a pickax, and the bonze collapsed immediately.

"I think it was the next day that one of the refugees,
Dr. Tan Sieng Eng, a doctor from Mongkol Borei
whom I used to know quite well, went to see the
Khmer Rouge to ask them for medication for the sick.
Because of this, the Khmer Rouge accused him of
being against the regime, of contesting it. They condemned the doctor to death through starvation. He
was kept a prisoner in one of the huts without food or
water until he was dead.

The fifth execution I witnessed was the worst. It
was the one of Tan Samay, a high school teacher from

Battambang. He was accused of being incapable of teaching properly. The only thing the children were being taught at the village was how to cultivate the soil. Maybe Tan Samay was trying to teach them other things, too, and that was his downfall. His pupils hanged him. A noose was passed around his neck; then the rope was passed over the branch of a tree. Half a dozen children between eight and ten years old held the loose end of the rope, pulling it sharply three or four times, dropping it in between. All the while they were shouting, 'Unfit teacher! Unfit teacher!' until Tan Samay was dead. The worst was that the children took obvious pleasure in killing."

From Ngy's work group, ten men were executed. Three were former army officers who upon arrival had naïvely told Comrade Mon the truth about their past. One morning soldiers appeared in the field and escorted them into the jungle. Later, in the jungle, Ngy saw their bodies—punctured by countless bullets. Children spies unmasked two police inspectors whom they overheard discussing their former work. Both were clubbed to death with hoes. Three more men also were killed with hoes after they complained about the lack of food.

A ninth man received a *kosang* for quarreling with his wife and another *kosang* after children heard him say, "This food isn't fit for pigs." Ngy did not know what his third offense was, but he and another man were put to death together outside the village.

On September 14 the committee ordered Ngy to patrol the village in the evening after the workday ended. He pleaded to be spared the added night duty, explaining that he was so weak he could barely work during the day. "I just cannot," he said. "After a day of work I simply have to rest." A few hours later *Angka* gave him the second *kosang*, which lasted more than an hour.

Recalling his previous laziness and derelictions, Comrade Mon shouted, "Stop going against the Wheel of History. Stop refusing orders given by *Angka Loeu*. There is no reason why you cannot do night duty."

"I made a mistake, and I am sorry," Ngy said. "I shall accept *Angka Loeu's* order." Comrade Mon congratulated him for realizing his error and cautioned him not to commit another. He did not have to explain why.

Ngy's brothers told his mother of the *kosang*, and upon returning to the hut, he found her near hysteria. "You must leave right away," she implored. "Please, for my sake, save your life. You know there won't be a third warning." Ngy was afraid for himself. But he also was afraid that without him, his mother and younger relatives would not long survive. Deliberating much of the night, he decided he could not abandon them.

Before his work group departed for the fields the next morning, a committee member casually mentioned that soldiers would accompany them. Ngy instantly knew what their presence meant. One or more members of the group were to be executed, and he suspected that during the night *Angka* had condemned him to death. He sneaked back to the hut, put some rubies and sapphires in his money belt and slipped the flute into his pants.

When all was ready, he crouched down in front of his mother and put her feet on his head for the traditonal Khmer benediction. "You were born on a

Monday," his mother sobbed. "You must leave on a Monday and you will live." The day was Monday.

The rain beat down torrentially as Ngy limped along the edge of the rice paddies, searching for a former soldier who secretly had been urging him to join in an escape attempt. Finally, he caught his friend's attention, and the two slipped off into the jungle, aware that they would be shot if caught more than 100 meters beyond the village perimeter. Threading their way through dense jungle all day, they advanced only 5 kilometers when darkness and exhaustion compelled them to stop for the night. According to rumors in the country, some tigers had developed a heightened craving for human flesh, having fed upon the many bodies around the New Villages. And Ngy's friend was so terrified of tigers that he insisted on sleeping in a tree. Unconcerned, Ngy slept on a fallen tree trunk until awakened by the growl and stench of a tiger nearby. He scurried up a tree and tied himself to a limb while the tiger prowled below.

VII

BROTHERS
AND SISTERS

Throughout that first season of horror, the summer and early autumn of 1975, the serfs of the New Villages looked to the coming harvest for some relief, if not complete deliverance, from their misery. They expected that at least they would share the rice forthcoming from fields created and cultivated with little other than their own bare hands. And they hoped that this product of their extraordinary labor would break the famine, restore their bodies and revitalize their defenses against disease. The harvest represented the one hope they realistically could harbor.

But in the autumn *Angka Loeu* once more convulsed the population by instituting, suddenly and inexplicably, a second great migration. With the harvest only weeks away, more than half a million men, women and children were lifted out of settlements they had built in the south and scattered anew to start all over again in the north and northwest. There, from other forests and jungles, they were to carve out and plant new lands without ever tasting a grain of the rice they had grown.

Ang Sokthan, the pharmaceutical student expelled from Phnom Penh on April 17, heard the second evacuation order at midnight on a moonlit September evening. Soldiers awakened her and all other inhabitants in the New Village of Phum Knar, situated in the jungles 64 kilometers south of Phnom Penh, and called them to a special meeting. "*Angka* wants you to leave this place and find another place to stay," they announced. "Go back and prepare to leave at once."

The soldiers offered the villagers not even a hint of why they had to leave or where they would go, and no one dared inquire. Ang, though, felt she must ask something in behalf of her older brothers, Kim, a twenty-five-year-old electronics engineer, and Tam, a twenty-three-year-old social worker. Experience had taught her never to speak a sentence that connoted complaint or protest, and she phrased her words carefully as she talked to one of the soldiers. Both of her brothers were suffering from hepatitis, malaria, beriberi and intestinal parasites, and their legs were so painfully swollen they could scarcely walk. Kim's condition was especially grave. Could an exception possibly be made in his case? Could he be allowed to stay in Phum Knar until after the harvest and regain his strength? And could she and her younger sister, Anna, who was nineteen, remain behind to help him? The soldier's reply was quick and direct. There would be no exceptions. "Prepare to leave at once."

Shortly afterward Kim, Tam, Ang and Anna started out on foot in the company of about 100 other families. They had to traverse 10 kilometers of jungle, thorny scrubland and marsh to reach National Highway 2, where trucks were supposed to pick them up; thus, there was time to talk and assess the future. The four young people were extremely close to one another. The children of farmers, they had grown up together outside Siem Reap, then had come to Phnom Penh to study at the university. The brothers, in both the country and the city, had always affectionately looked after their sisters. Ang and Anna in turn loved and idolized their brothers, and during the bitter summer they had tried to nurse and protect them in every way they could, even giving them part of their own inadequate rice ration. All four were united in determination that whatever the adversity, they would remain together and survive together.

Walking under the moonlight, Kim suggested that the new migration might be a blessing. In Phum Knar they had toiled in the fields through rain and sun from 5:30 A.M. to 5:30 P.M. and on moonlit nights from 7 to 10 P.M. As work sites were moved farther and farther away, they had to arise as early as 2 A.M. to be at work on time. Ang and hundreds of other women carried baskets of dirt on their heads for construction of a big dike in the paddies. The long, silent lines of women trudging back and forth reminded her of a colony of black ants. Food rations were halved in June and dropped well below starvation levels, and cholera, malaria and dysentery claimed a heavy toll. Kim reasoned that nowhere could their life be worse and that perhaps at their next destination medicine might be available. Speaking objectively, rather than indulging in self-pity, he remarked, "If we do not get some Western medicine, we are going to die."

They arrived at the highway shortly after dawn, only to be informed that the trucks had not come and they must return to the settlement. Twice again in the next ten days they plodded through the night from the settlement to the highway, and the trucks were not there. On October 2, when they repeated the trek a fourth time, Kim and Tam were so weak that they required the support of their sisters to walk. This time, though, they waited, and after half a day a long convoy of Chinese trucks appeared.

Their truck contained about eighty people, so jammed together that no one could sit, much less lie down. Many were as enfeebled as Kim and Tam, but the children were the most pitiable of all. To Ang they looked like pictures of starving Indian children she had seen in some of her pharmacy classes. Their limbs were like matchsticks, their stomachs were bloated, the dark portions of their eyes were turning white and their eyes were so sensitive to light that it hurt to open them in sunlight.

The convoy traveled northward and, heading toward Pursat, passed through a section of Phnom Penh. During the half hour or so they were in the capital Ang saw only about twenty people, all soldiers. Phnom Penh University appeared wholly deserted, and she heard not a sound. After being on the road some thirty hours, during which there was one rest stop, the trucks at midday discharged their passengers in a field opposite the Pursat railway station. For some the journey was too much. During the next few hours Ang saw a number of people die in the field, and others, lying helplessly on the ground unable to talk or move, obviously were about to die. There were no shovels, no place, no time for burial, and the bereaved paid their last respects to loved ones by partially covering the bodies with sleeping mats.

At sundown an engine pulling a train of freight cars that stretched over the horizon chugged into the station. Because of heavy rain driven by cold winds, the people rushed to climb into the freight cars. However, the cars were high off the ground, there were no ladders and Ang and Anna in the shoving crowds exhausted themselves pulling their now-delirious brothers aboard. So many men, women—all dirty, many sick—crammed the freight cars that no one could lie down to sleep, and for some reason the train did not move all night. To relieve themselves, people had to climb down and go into the field. In the darkness, an eight-year-old boy fell into a pond and ran back screaming. Attached to his leg were big leeches.

The train departed at nine o'clock in the morning, moving slowly northwestward. Many people, having shivered through the night, fainted in the sweltering daytime heat, and not a drop of water was available. In midafternoon they rolled through Battambang, formerly Cambodia's second largest city, and so far as Ang could see, it was even more devoid of life than Phnom Penh. Atop all their other ailments, Kim and Tam that afternoon began to suffer from diarrhea and high fever. Unable to offer them food, water or medicine, Ang and Anna attempted to comfort them with words and the touch of their hands.

Late in the afternoon the train stopped in Sisophon, everybody was ordered off and for the first time since April 17 Ang observed some gestures of official compassion. Waiting were jugs of water and an *Angka* reception committee composed of about thirty civilians and armed soldiers, male and female. They seemed relaxed and evinced none of the familiar homicidal harshness, the unmistakable readiness to shoot on caprice. *Angka* explained that all families would be dispatched to the fields, but that single persons had the option of working in the countryside or performing unspecified duties for *Angka*. Ang, Kim, Tam and Anna held a council, and their initial inclination was to go into the countryside in hope that they would be assigned to an area around Siem Reap where they might find their parents. They concluded, though, that further travel would be fatal to Kim and Tam and that they should volunteer to serve *Angka Loeu* on the chance that they could thereby remain together and obtain medical care. Unwisely, Ang told the truth about her background, and she was rejected—*Angka Loeu* did not need educated people.

Then the miraculous happened. Upon seeing Kim and Tam, half-conscious, desperately holding onto their sisters to keep from falling down, an official directed that they be sent to a clinic. And at seven o'clock the next evening Ang and Anna were summoned from the field to which they had been assigned outside Sisophon and told to report to the hospital to attend to their brothers! To Ang, the only explanation was that Buddha and the spirits of her ancestors had interceded.

At the old brick hospital the brothers were treated with injections of Western medicine. Although she had studied pharmacy for three years, Ang could not discern what the medicine was or whether it was appropriate, and neither was she sure that the very young medical staff, all dressed in black, included any bona fide physicians. Nevertheless, the hospital provided patients with all the food they desired, and

both Kim and Tam seemed to grow stronger and better. But by the tenth day their steady improvement
had ended, perhaps because the malfunctioning of
their livers began to affect the hearts, and their condition quickly deteriorated. And the two sisters, who for
months had been constantly exposed to innumerable
diseases without ever becoming seriously sick, now,
in the hospital, were incapacitated by violent
stomach disorders. Just as all four most needed
genuine treatment, they were removed, again without
explanation, from the hospital and placed in another
institution known as Zone 5 Hospital.

Here, in former school buildings, were lodged
about 1,000 bedridden patients. Ang by now thought
she had become inured to every conceivable kind of
filth, and she even could excuse its presence in the
primitive New Village. But what she saw in the hospital was to her incredible. Classrooms and corridors
were packed with soiled beds pushed closely to one
another, thereby accelerating the spread of conta-
gious diseases. Serum was stored in Coca-Cola and
Pepsi-Cola bottles, and liquid potions of every de-
scription, including herb medicines, were kept in
used penicillin bottles. Most of the "doctors" and
other personnel were illiterate. They made no effort to
diagnose the ills of individual patients, treating
everyone with the same mishmash of pills, herb con-
coctions and homemade serum. They administered injections with unsterilized needles so ineptly and
brutally that a majority of patients Ang saw had
abscesses. Once when Tam was shouting in delirious
pain, an unnerved "doctor" bent over him and yelled,
"We can't help you! We don't have any medicine."

Kim knew he was dying. Toward the end he could

only stare vacantly at his sisters and faintly squeeze their hands. When he died, his body was dumped into a cart along with the other dead of the day and, as Ang and Anna watched, trundled away toward a communal burial pit.

Three days later, when Ang returned to the hospital with a fish she had caught in the river for Tam, his bed was empty. "Oh, he's dead," she was told "We've already buried him."

The rage and bitterness of the sisters almost equaled their grief. "They treated them like animals, like cats or dogs they kill in the streets," Ang sobbed when she and Anna were alone.

While bathing at the river, Ang had met a forty-year-old farmer and his daughter. Confident of the sisters' hatred of *Angka Loeu* and sympathizing with them, the farmer shortly after Tam's death made a secret overture. An attempt to escape from Cambodia was being plotted. He was in touch with some bandits who knew hidden routes through the jungles to Thailand. In return for a payment the bandits would lead Ang and Anna to freedom. If the girls elected to join the attempt, they were to accompany his daughter on November 12 to a designated hut in the village of Kiep 5 kilometers down the road toward Mongkol Borei. From there the escape party, composed of his whole family and others, would depart. With their brothers dead, the whereabouts and fate of their parents unknown, the girls instantly agreed.

The thirty or so people who rendezvoused at the edge of Kiep on the twelfth were, with the exception of Ang and Anna, all farmers and their families. There were five bandits, all in their late twenties, wearing khaki bush jackets and armed. They looked like the hardened criminal adventurers they were. To one, Ang gave Kim's expensive watch, which she had kept for him ever since leaving Phnom Penh because girls were less rigorously searched than men.

They set off at dark and walked until just before dawn. While the chief of the bandits took up a position as lookout, they lay down among rice plants, intending to hide there until nightfall. No sooner had they settled than a baby among them began to bawl loudly. The lookout shouted, "They're over there!" With a communist patrol closing fast, everyone ran in a different direction.

Ang and Anna followed the chief of the bandits and one of his lieutenants deep into the forest, and the four buried themselves in thick underbrush until dark. Pushing on the second night, Ang three times cut her foot on sharp thorns, and by dawn she was in pain and exhausted. But they now were on a mountain where the bandits judged it relatively safe to move in daylight, and the two men wanted to press on because they were far behind schedule and had food enough for only three days. Ang did her best, yet her injured foot and general weakness so slowed the advance that the younger bandit announced he was going on alone. Although the chief stayed behind with the girls, Ang sensed that he was apprehensive and wanted to desert them. She knew that if he did, both Anna and she certainly would die.

In the afternoon Ang began to cry. She thought of the deaths of Kim and Tam and the prospect of Anna dying on the mountain with her. Her reserves were gone; she simply had no strength to continue. Only if she dropped out now could her sister live. She called, "Anna, go on. I can't walk any longer."

Anna pleaded with her. "You've come this far. There are only ten kilometers to go. Try a little longer." Ang tried, but over the next few hundred meters she fell down repeatedly and each time had to be picked up.

Finally, the bandit spoke, kindly but realistically. "We don't have any more food or water," he said, "and on this mountain it's very difficult to find water. I have tried to help you all I could. I can't help you anymore. If I stay with you, we must all die."

Ang pulled from her pockets and underwear all the valuables they had managed to retain—a ring, a necklace, a bracelet, a purse of American coins totaling about $20, some Japanese and Chinese currency. Handing all to the bandit, she said, "Please look after my sister. Please help her across the border."

Too overcome to speak, Ang and Anna held each other tightly and wept. Anna could not bring herself to part from her sister's embrace. Then Ang saw the bandit begin to move away, and she pushed her sister toward him. Though on the verge of fainting, she watched until they disappeared from sight into the mountain foliage. Utterly spent and forlorn, Ang now prepared for death by collapsing into profound sleep.

She awoke in the morning strangely refreshed, serene and unafraid. She reasoned that the worst that could happen to her had happened and resolved that if she must die, then she would go forward and meet death rather than cravenly lie back and await it. She imagined that she was in a garden full of fragrant flowers instead of a forest hostile with sharp bamboo and predatory animals. She was not alone, but surrounded by good and gentle friends.

Knowing only that Thailand lay to the west, she

walked in the direction opposite the sunrise. When she tired, she rested; when she was sleepy, she lay down, prayed to Buddha and the spirits of her brothers, then slept. She found no food but learned to satisfy her thirst by licking dew from the foliage, and once she came upon the hollow stump of a tree filled with water. Folding a leaf into a cup, she drank deeply, and the water was delicious.

By the eighth day of her solitary flight Ang, moving mostly at night, had made her way past a mountain she had been heading for and found herself on a cattle trail which she guessed was used by smugglers operating on the Thailand-Cambodian border. When the moon came out, she saw a rice field—another good sign because in the eight days she had seen no rice. The barking of a dog suggested that a village was nearby. But was the village Thai or Cambodian?

She slept until daylight, then hid by a trail to observe. Four men, two carrying knives, passed, but the knives scared her, so she stayed hidden. A little while later, two men—one middle-aged, the other younger—walked by, unarmed and carrying baskets of fish. Ang decided to take the chance.

She ran out, grabbed the older man by the hand and said, "I'm Cambodian. I've just escaped from Cambodia." Both men looked startled, and understandably so. Before them stood a figure that was little more than a skeleton, coated with dried blood and dirt. "Is she human?" the younger man asked. He spoke in Thai. Ang was free.

In the refugee camp at Aranyaprathet Ang diligently inquired of all other Cambodians who recently had preceded her across the border, in an effort to discover what had happened to her sister. Ultimately she learned that the bandit who took Anna from the mountain had stepped on a communist land mine near the border. He was badly hurt but managed to crawl into Thailand. Behind he left a body which the explosion had dismembered beyond recognition.

VIII

THE
HUNTED

They finally caught Sergeant Major Sem Vann on
August 10, and he knew they were going to kill him,
probably not with bullets.

After seeing the bodies of the massacred officers at
Mount Tippadei in April, Sem fled southeast toward
Takeo in an attempt to rejoin his parents, whom he
had not seen since enlisting in the army eight years
before. Midway between Battambang and Phnom
Penh, however, he was forced off the highway and
ordered to a New Village deep in the forest. On June
15 soldiers summoned villagers from the rice paddies
to announce that there was no more food. "Comrades,
you must understand that the only way to carry rice to
us is by oxcart. That takes time, of course." Three men
evidently complained, and the next day soldiers
broke their necks with hoes. That night Sem and six
other villagers rendezvoused under a tree and decided to try to escape from Cambodia.

By now anyone traveling required an *Angka Loeu*

pass. Though later the passes were to become more sophisticated in form, they still were crude—slips of ordinary paper on which village chieftains authorized travel to a specified native village. Thus, it was easy for one of Sem's fellow conspirators, who retained pencil and paper, to forge a pass empowering them to proceed to a village in northwestern Cambodia.

Patrols on the highway toward Battambang routinely honored the pass, and one even gave the party a lift in a trailer pulled by a tractor. But east of Battambang a communist officer, indifferent to what anyone else might have authorized, ordered them hauled away to a New Village called Prey Damrei. Upon arrival, they were told, "Whoever tries to escape will be shot." In a period of six weeks Sem saw at least fifteen people die of disease or starvation. In early August he and four friends escaped again.

A week later they were jumped by a patrol on the road outside Mongkol Borei, 55 kilometers from the Thai border. They might have been shot out of hand had not the communists been so worried about the increasing activity of an underground movement led by former Prime Minister In Tam. The communists suspected that Sem, whose handsome military bearing made him look like an officer, was an agent of In Tam, and they wanted to wrench out all he knew before disposing of him.

Sem and his four friends were locked in a makeshift jail, a frame structure with barred windows. The cell walls were made of tightly woven palm leaves, which sufficed to restrain prisoners but did not block sound. At about 4 A.M. their first night in jail they heard an interrogation being conducted in a nearby cell.

A voice weakly said, "Yes, I was in the military."

"What rank?"

"Sergeant."

"No! You are a liar! You are an officer in In Tam's army!"

Sem heard some muted, anguished sounds whose meaning he could not decipher. Then the prisoner pleaded, "No, it's the truth. If I'm lying, kill me and kill my whole family."

"No need to kill your family. It will be enough just to kill you."

Later that morning Sem and his friends overheard a communist soldier of no more than twelve talking to their guard. "I won't be able to eat anything today," the boy said tremulously.

"Why not?" asked the guard.

"Because this morning I saw somebody killed with a pickax. He wasn't quite dead, so others came and finished him off with sticks."

In combat Sem had often been beset by fear, which he overcame with courage. Young, bright, vigorous, he very much wanted to live, yet as a soldier he was ready to give up his life for his beliefs. But the prospect of dying in degradation, of being hacked to death with an ax, simultaneously sickened and outraged him. Berating himself for having surrendered at Battambang, he now resolved to fight as long as he breathed.

He searched the cell looking for a way to break out, and there seemed to him only one way. The window frame was made of boards, and if the lower supporting board could be pried loose, it might be possible to crawl out. Among them, they had one tool—a fingernail clipper. Whenever their guard was out of sight, they worked feverishly, taking turns gouging out wood from around the nails so they could pull out the nails. After six hours of scraping and tugging, the first nail came out. Although their fingers were raw and numb, they knew they had a chance—if they had enough time before *Angka Loeu* finished with them.

At about 5 P.M. on the second day the board moved. They waited until darkness and rain descended, then one by one squeezed out into the night. For the next five days and nights they pressed due westward through the jungle, never stopping for more than half an hour and keeping away from all trails. They had nothing to eat, nothing to help them except determination. But on the sixth morning their fortitude delivered them into a tiny village where the signs were printed in Thai.

For every Cambodian such as Sem Vann, Ang Sokthan, Tevi Rosa or Ly Bun Heng who succeeded in escaping, many more died trying to flee. Nothing so provoked the wrath and cruelty of *Angka Loeu* as an escape attempt. People merely suspected of wanting to escape were executed. Men, women and children apprehended while running away were put to death with especial barbarism. *Kosangs,* or warnings, might be given for other offenses. Escapees rarely received a second chance.

On April 17 *Angka Loeu* began sealing off the entire border with Thailand—a 720-kilometer frontier that curves through mountains, jungles, rivers and forests, stretching from beyond the 1,000-year-old temple ruins of Preah Vihear in the north to Klong Yai, a fishing town in Thailand's remote southeastern province of Trat. Villages and settlements were evacuated to create a no-man's-land about 5 kilometers wide all along the border and blockades erected on all roads leading toward Thailand. An array of deadly obstacles was installed along the frontier, and the odds against successful escape progressively lengthened.

The communists seeded border crossings, their approaches and jungle trails with hundreds of thousands of mines and booby traps fashioned from grenades. Phal Oudam, the thirty-one-year-old philosophy professor, slipped out of the disease-ridden village of Sambok Ork, 30 kilometers southeast of Poipet, on the evening of September 4, 1975. With five other men, he headed into the jungle toward Thailand. They had walked along a trail perhaps an hour when a booby trap exploded underfoot, injuring four of them.

"The two of us who were uninjured gave a hand to the wounded, each of us supporting two persons. It was about seven P.M., very dark and raining. I helped my two charges for another hundred meters or so until I tripped over something. There was a strange noise—chhhhh! Instinctively I threw myself on the ground, but my companions were not so quick. A grenade exploded upward from the ground, hitting one in the head, the other in the chest, and killing both instantly.

"By this time I had lost contact with the other three men. All I could hear was the noise of two more explosions in the darkness."

Realizing he was caught in a minefield, Phal dared not take another step in the darkness, and he climbed a tree, holding onto a thick branch throughout the night. At dawn he looked down on a grisly scene.

"I could see countless groups of bodies, five, ten meters apart, with the corpses piled on top of each other. As I picked my way along the track, I saw more corpses. Some swollen bodies; some only skeletons. Groups of five bodies, twenty bodies, three bodies, two bodies. The Khmer Rouge would plant two sticks in the ground, then tie a string between them to the grenades' firing pins. If you walked carefully, you could see the traps, but at night it was impossible. At an abandoned village, Prasath Rang, about twenty kilometers from the border, I saw between two hundred and three hundred corpses. There were many trails leading in and out of this village. The Khmer Rouge had placed booby traps all along the trails, and refugees who passed this way died. Their bodies were all over the place."

Young Phorn, a former policeman, stumbled upon another kind of trap laid in the jungles by *Angka Loeu*. Increasingly in the autumn of 1975 New Villagers heard rumors that *Angka Loeu* planned to massacre all former soldiers and civil servants, regardless of rank, after the harvest. On October 30, fearing execution, Young and a friend fled New Village No. 32, located some 50 kilometers east of Pailin.

"Before reaching the border, we crossed a trail in the jungle. Nearby was a huge heap of bodies, all in civilian clothing. There were so many I couldn't accurately estimate their number. We had had a moment of panic there when we felt a Khmer Rouge ambush was nearby. But just as we were about to run, we noticed harpoonlike barbed spears made of metal sticking out of the ground. Investigating, we discovered wooden boards, about 300 centimeters long, had been buried in the ground. Each board was studded with about ten such harpoons. The metal was so sharp that it would pierce any rubber sandal or canvas shoe, such as most

Cambodians are wearing. Maybe the bodies nearby were people who had walked into these awful traps, then were unable to continue and were killed by the Khmer Rouge on the spot."

The communists also set ambushes in those hospitable areas where fatigued families might be tempted to rest or seek water. Chheng Savan, a gem prospector, hoped to drink from a large pool known as the Pond of Forty Crocodiles north of Pailin. "Approaching it, there was again this strong smell of putrefaction. Soon we saw a female body in an advanced stage of decomposition, bones showing in parts. We knew it was a woman because of the long hair. Closer to the pond there were at least twenty more bodies, all in the same stage of putrefaction. The pond was an ideal spot for an ambush." Later, at a camp in Thailand, Chheng encountered refugees who told him that they indeed had been ambushed while drinking at the Pond of Forty Crocodiles and that more than thirty of their party were killed.

Throughout the border region *Angka Loeu* patrols armed with machine guns, rockets, mortars and grenades roamed the jungles and mountains, hunting escapees like animals. Keo Kim Taun, a former government soldier, was one of thirty-seven people who tried to escape to Thailand from the village of Soeur. A patrol spotted them cooking rice in a forest clearing and opened fire with AK-47 machine guns, killing twenty-one men, women and children, the youngest of whom was five. Keo and the other fifteen survivors, several of them wounded, reached Thailand twelve days later. En route they saw remains of innumerable people slaughtered by other patrols. Keo came upon the corpses of eight adults and children who were bound together. He guessed they composed a family which had been tied together and marched across a land mine.

Tue Piey and nearly 300 other peasants fled en masse from a village outside Battambang in January 1976. Only he and eleven others lived through the attacks by various patrols who fired at them on the way to Thailand. The same month Thai authorities announced that Cambodian troops pursuing a party of refugees crossed into Thailand after them and gunned twenty-three persons to death.

Thirty kilometers from the border rockets were fired at a group of 106 people who had crossed the By Ban Noy Mountain. The initial salvos hit no one, but the refugees scattered in panic and hid in underbrush. While a communist patrol searched for them, three babies—two of them three months old and one, six months—began to cry. Fearful that the cries would bring down a rain of rockets upon everyone, the fathers of the infants each independently made the same terrible decision. Each strangled his own child.

When the people resumed their flight, two mothers with small children lagged behind. Soldiers caught up with them and killed eleven children, four from one family, seven from the other. The mothers, quicker to hide than the children, got away and later rejoined the main party.

In addition to the lethal barriers erected by *Angka Loeu*, the jungles themselves posed a formidable obstacle to escape. They are not the lush tropical rain forests of romantic fiction, resplendent with cool azure pools, multicolored vegetation and exotic fruit. Rather, the jungles of western Cambodia are a hostile wilderness of banyan trees, thorny bushes, sharp bamboo, poisonous plants, barren scrubland and savanna. They are inhabited by mosquitoes, leeches, crocodiles, tigers, elephants, wild oxen, panthers, bears and reptiles, including cobras, constrictors and kraits. Strong people can subsist in them for a time, as smugglers and brigands have done for centuries. But they resist prolonged human habitation, and in their way the jungles were just as pitiless toward the bedraggled men, women and children who ventured into them as was *Angka Loeu.*

Yet despite all the deathly dangers of the traps, the patrols, the jungles, the will of the people to be free of *Angka Loeu* was so powerful and inextinguishable that each month thousands tried to escape. Although people from the lower socioeconomic strata always composed the majority of refugees, the first waves included a disproportionate number of students, intellectuals, prosperous tradesmen, civil servants and military personnel. But by August 1975, as Jon Swain reported in the London *Sunday Times,* the overwhelming proportion was made up of "humble country folk, recognizable by the heavy tattooing of their bodies, dark skins and coarse hands and feet—the people one would think best suited for the rigors of peasant revolution."

Regardless of background, all who tried to escape after the first month or so of communist domination set out with the knowledge that they were beginning a life-or-death duel with *Angka Loeu.* The soldiers of *Angka Loeu* were veritably swathed in military weapons. Against them the people had to employ the weapons of courage, ingenuity and daring.

One man who knew how to use such weapons was Chen Yed, a thirty-eight-year-old former army sergeant. Stocky and powerfully built, Chen was quick-thinking, decisive, and competent, and although he adopted the mannerisms of a farmer to avoid retribution, his personal qualities still brought him to the attention of *Angka*. In establishing the New Villages, the communists tried to appoint as chieftains and administrators people identified as their supporters. However, they had so comparatively few supporters and there were so many villages that they often had to pick the unknown—who in any case were constantly supervised by soldiers and the district committee of *Angka*. Though mystified, Chen had no choice but to accept when *Angka* designated him president of the Sala Krau labor district, comprised of three New Villages situated northeast of Poipet 28 kilometers from Thailand.

In August 1975 Sala Krau was a microcosm of new Democratic Cambodia. The rice ration was down to famine level, some fifteen people had been shot while trying to escape, a number of men believed to have been in the military had been "sent to *Angka Loeu*" and roughly 30 percent of the people were completely incapacitated, awaiting death, which in the circumstances Chen felt would be merciful. On August 8 one of the four communist soldiers permanently assigned to the district confided that soon *Angka Loeu* would issue a list of villagers "required for special work projects" elsewhere. The names the soldier mentioned convinced Chen that a new and more intense pogrom against former military personnel and civil servants, as well as their wives and children, was in the offing.

Thinking back on how his people had been killed off one by one by *Angka Loeu,* Chen conceived an idea. Although the terror of *Angka Loeu* was everywhere, its forces were spread thin. If the four guards stationed in Sala Krau were killed in the afternoon or early evening, the whole population could disappear without being missed until morning. And if a new, secret trail could be charted through the forest, the whole population could be near the Thai border before *Angka Loeu* could organize pursuit.

Among the inhabitants of Sala Krau was a former government forestry employee named Ban who had worked years in the surrounding terrain. Promising to cover his absence, Chen dispatched him to prepare the escape route by marking a trail through the 28 kilometers of forest to Thailand. Next, he approached each member of the governing *Angka* committee, which was composed of the three village chiefs and eighteen leaders of work groups. Any one of them could have assured himself a favored position in Democratic Cambodia by betraying Chen and the plan. None did. And even though a few considered the scheme suicidal, all pledged to act upon receipt of Chen's signal.

On August 14 the list of people Chen was to deliver up to *Angka Loeu* for execution arrived unexpectedly. If they were to be saved, the break would have to be made that night.

The Sala Krau district was divided by a small river, and the four guards customarily split into pairs, each patrolling one side of the stream. At 11 A.M. Chen sent two of his best men, both former soldiers, to hunt down the guards on the side of the river distant from the main village. At about 3 P.M. they found their quarry still resting from the midday break, snatched their rifles and killed them both.

Chen and his brother-in-law went after the other two guards that evening, locating them in a pagoda which the communists had converted into a barracks and office. The guards were unaware of the fate of their comrades and somewhat distracted by three communist nurses who had come to survey health conditions in Sala Krau. Accustomed to conferring with Chen, they discerned nothing unusual in his visit and left their rifles leaning against the wall. Chen and the brother-in-law chatted with them, poised for the moment when they looked away. When it came, they grabbed the rifles and started shooting, riddling both soldiers in the chest.

The three nurses ran out of the pagoda, screaming. Waiting confederates of Chen seized the women and gave them a simple choice: come with us or die. Now committee members passed the word throughout the village that the time to flee had come. At 9 P.M. 1,806 villagers, plus the 3 captive nurses, marched out of Sala Krau in an orderly column led by forester Ban and Chen.

Ban had done his job brilliantly, marking a sinuous trail through rarely traveled areas where patrols were least likely to be encountered. Chen interspersed stronger men along the column to help the weak and carry anyone who collapsed. He had resolved that all would live or die together, that not a single man, woman or child would be abandoned. Under a full moon the column silently snaked its way through the forest with people taking turns holding small children and aiding the elderly. Throughout the night they met no one, and at dawn they could see Thailand. At 10:30 A.M. all 1,806 crossed the border.

Chen asked the first Thai he saw for directions to

the nearest pagoda and, without even a brief pause for rest, immediately led the column to it. Although food was their most precious material possession, the people in the Buddhist tradition offered what they had to the monks in thanksgiving for their deliverance. Afterward many crowded around Chen and proclaimed him a hero. "We are reborn!" some shouted. "We are reborn!"

For those lodged in the interior, the risks and difficulties of escape were, of course, much greater, and as the controls of *Angka Loeu* tightened, they became almost insuperable. Of all the myriad attempts to flee from the heartland, the most audacious recorded was made by four young men—Dap Youn, twenty-six, his brother, Dap Nim, seventeen, and two friends, Sam Son, twenty-one, and Sam An, eighteen.

After the exodus from Phnom Penh, Dap Youn and Dap Nim settled in the village of Tuol Speu, about 30 kilometers to the south. There Dap Youn prudently concealed the fact that he had been a soldier. But Dap Nim truthfully stated he was a photographer, and in June *Angka Loeu* suddenly ordered him to Phnom Penh to take propaganda pictures. In the ghostly capital, Dap Nim lived as a semiprisoner, surrounded by communist soldiers, in a house with a darkroom and studio. Dap Youn labored in the village through the summer, watching people die daily, sharing the common travail and hunger of the living.

On the night of November 12 Dap Youn heard a voice softly calling outside his hut. It was Dap Nim, who motioned him to follow into the darkness. Half-crouching, the brothers sneaked out of the village and down the road to a parked Peugeot 404 sedan. Sitting inside were Sam Son and Sam An, both auto

mechanics drafted to work in an *Angka* motor pool. Dap Nim had become friends with them, and the three had connived to steal the Peugeot, pick up Dap Youn in Tuol Speu, then escape to Thailand. Their plan was to drive to Nimit, near Sisophon, abandon the car and contact smuggler acquaintances, who could lead them along secret routes to the border.

Heading north toward Phnom Penh, they realized that the diesel-driven Peugeot was so slow they probably would be overtaken if pursued. But Sam Son said he could easily steal a larger, faster automobile. The motor pool behind the old Soriya Cinema was unguarded because the communists believed they had immobilized the cars kept there by draining the tanks.

To garb and equip themselves for flight, the four stopped in Phnom Penh at Nim's house, which served as a barracks and photo center. While Dap Youn hid in the car outside and the soldiers slept inside the house, Dap Nim and the Sams scooped up all available supplies that could be used for bribes or sold in Thailand. Their loot included American rice, canned food, eight cameras, cigarettes, a compass, an AK-47 rifle and a Smith & Wesson pistol. They also stole military clothing for Dap Youn and took along two extra dress-green uniforms.

At the motor pool Sam Son and Sam An chose a 1975 cream-colored Mercedes, whose odometer showed it had been driven less than 4,800 kilometers. Out of jerry cans taken from *Angka Loeu* stocks to which they had access, Sam Son poured the tank full of gas and loaded three extra cans of fuel into the sedan.

Dressed in the black shirts, black trousers, Ho Chi Minh sandals and scarves of communist soldiers, the

four left at 2 A.M., speeding through the desolate capital toward Battambang. Approaching a checkpoint on
Highway 5, they prepared for searching interrogation. But here and at subsequent checkpoints, soldiers, instead of halting them, respectfully waved
them on. Doubtless the guards reasoned that as only
Angka could have the best, such an elegant car must
represent *Angka Loeu*. The Mercedes became a magic
carpet, wafting the conspirators in a few hours over
distances it had taken millions weeks to walk. About
6 A.M. they entered Battambang, still a wasteland, and
here again, none of the patrols had the temerity to
challenge them.

Dap Youn was the first to perceive the opportunity.
Why try to struggle on foot through the jungles when,
as important emissaries of *Angka Loeu*, they could
drive to Poipet, crash through the bamboo barrier on
the border bridge and ride into Thailand in style?
Assuming the airs of an *Angka Loeu* dignitary, he
instructed Sam An to don one of the dress-green uniforms such as *Angka* drivers wore and become their
official chauffeur.

Outside Battambang they slowed at a barricade
guarded by grim female soldiers, and Dap Youn
sensed that the women were not inclined to let the car
pass unchecked. Quickly he told the "chauffeur" to
stop before they were ordered to do so. "Take a camera, and start shooting pictures," he whispered to Dap
Nim.

To the girl soldiers Dap Youn announced, "*Angka*
has sent us to make a movie of happy peasants toiling
in the fields. Yesterday we were in Sihanoukville.
Today it is your turn to be honored." Dap Nim swung
a movie camera left and right, jumping all about,

while Dap Youn issued commands to his brother and the workers laboring in adjoining fields. "Try this angle! Now this one! Smile as you work! *Angka* wants you to look happy!"

The corporeal presence of *Angka Loeu* so awed the girls that they asked neither for credentials nor for further explanation. Dap Youn airily inquired about the route to Nimit, and they respectfully pointed the way. Climbing back into the Mercedes, Sam Son resumed his role as chauffeur, and Sam An in the front seat assumed the pose of a bodyguard, conspicuously laying the AK-47 across his knees.

The closer to Thailand they drove, the stricter the controls became, and they were halted repeatedly between Battambang and Sisophon. But whenever a soldier hesitated, Dap Nim waved the camera, and Dap Youn imperiously said, "Smile please! *Angka Loeu* wants you to look happy."

At a roadblock in Sisophon, though, it appeared that the spell cast by the Mercedes and their pretensions might be fatally broken. Another squad of female soldiers challenged them, and one coldly declared, "You can't travel north of here. You are not showing the proper license plates." The declaration shocked and frightened. Only now did they realize that the 1975 plates on the Mercedes had been invalidated by new licenses the communists issued after the conquest.

Dap Youn invented swiftly. "*Angka* needs movies of our patriotic workers as soon as possible," he said. "The French car assigned to me has broken down and is being repaired. *Angka Loeu* has given me this car, for our mission is so urgent we could not wait."

The young soldiers seemed almost satisfied, but

one remained just skeptical enough to ask for their papers. Dap Youn produced an *Angka* "Letter of Permission," a travel authorization forged on an official form by Nim. As the girls clustered around, one exclaimed, "It doesn't carry an *Angka* seal!"

Here they were most vulnerable. If anyone of intelligence dwelled upon the pass, they were lost. Dap Youn could think of nothing to do but magnify the lie. "Of course, it doesn't carry a seal from *Angka* or from *Angka Loeu*," he said patronizingly. "The people who sent us are from the highest *Angka* of them all, one so high that their passes don't *need* seals!"

The leader of the squad now was unsure of herself. "I'll show it to my chief," she said, taking the paper and walking away. While his companions ostentatiously swung cameras about and talked Khmer Rouge slang with the female soldiers, Dap Youn chatted with a male soldier who wandered up to the car. In the most comradely manner he could feign, he handed the young soldier four or five packages of cigarettes. The youth, who probably had not had a cigarette in a long while, was utterly delighted. Gazing at the sky, Dap Youn in exasperation remarked in effect that if they were delayed too long in reaching their destination, falling shadows would preclude photography.

The female squad leader returned, apparently having been unable to find her chief. Before she could say anything, the bribed soldier spoke up. "Let them drive on. Soon it will be too late to take pictures. You'll check on them tomorrow. They have to pass through here on their way back to Phnom Penh. So let them do their job."

The Mercedes rolled into Poipet about 2 P.M., and

shortly afterward they neared the bridge that crosses the narrow Khlang Luk River into Thailand. But instead of the slender bamboo barrier they expected to see on the bridge, passage was blocked by a thick, strongly built wooden wall and farther on by two huge trucks. They had no choice except to repeat their act until discovering means of crossing the river.

Leaving the car, Dap Youn authoritatively explained their moviemaking mission to a skeptical commander of the communist border guard, a bulky man with a round, mean face. To Dap Youn at that moment it was never more obvious that the four of them were impostors. But after wavering between duty and fear of *Angka Loeu*, the commander ordered the entire border guard, some 100 men, to line up for photographs.

The brothers staged quite a show, alternately taking group pictures and individual shots. They kept searching for a chance to slip away to the river, but the soldiers were always too close.

"We've got to do something," Dap Youn muttered to his brother.

"We'll pretend the lens cover is lost and ask if we can look for it," Dap Nim answered. While the rest of the guard dispersed, two soldiers were detailed to help in the search. The Daps and the Sams led them into a tedious exercise, crawling around on hands and knees, cursing their negligence and the shortage of camera parts, slowly edging toward the river. Finally, one of the soldiers said, "You keep looking. We have to go back."

Once the soldiers were out of sight, the four scampered down the riverbank and hopped into a rowboat, probably used to smuggle rice from Thailand. In less

than a minute they were on the opposite shore. Their
journey to freedom had taken little more than sixteen
hours.

Few were so fortunate. Phim Uon, one of the four
known survivors of the Mount Tippadei massacre in
April, lived in hiding for the next eight months. For
weeks he nursed his wounds in the jungle, then took
refuge with a grandmother near Sisophon. When a
search party came looking for him, he pried up floor-
ing, slid out underneath the house and got away. Subsequently he hid under an assumed name with relatives in the village of Trabek. There, in late November,
he was reunited with his thirteen-year-old son, who
had made his way to Trabek to be with the relatives.
Villagers had told the boy that the communists,
searching for Phim, had taken away and slaughtered
his wife, his other children and grandchildren.
Knowing that the boy too would be killed if caught,
Phim led him into the jungle toward Thailand.

They considered themselves lucky when, on their
second day, they met forty other refugees being
guided toward the border by three armed members of
the anticommunist underground. Not long afterward
troops attacked the party with a fierce barrage, and
only seventeen survived. Separated from the others,
Phim and his son continued on alone. On December
11 they saw a jungle outpost which Phim guessed
might be manned by resistance fighters. Leaving the
boy behind, he scouted ahead alone until determin-
ing that the outpost was communist. With ten soldiers
pursuing them, he and his son ran about 500 meters
before exhaustion forced them to drop into tall grass
by the trail. Seeing that two of the soldiers had spotted
him, Phim got up, raised his arms in surrender and
walked off, hoping to decoy the troops away from the

boy and thereby save his life. As the soldiers started to tie him up, he pulled a knife from his belt, stabbed them both as viciously as he could and broke away. He concealed himself until darkness, then spent the night trying to find the boy. But now his son and whole family were gone. Sadly, Phim crossed into Thailand on December 13. Because he was dressed in black, Thai border guards thought he was a communist, so they beat and kicked him, then threw him in jail.*

Nhek Kem was a forty-six-year-old farmer who had lived all his life near Poipet until the communists drove him, his wife, four children and other relatives

---

*At a Thai camp in July 1976 a Cambodian refugee, who declined to divulge his true name on grounds that he was a member of the anticommunist underground, told François Ponchaud the following story.

In April 1976 Major Phim and six other former Cambodian officers or soldiers slipped back into Cambodia. Their mission was to contact representatives of the resistance movement in the Battambang-Maung Russei area. En route back to Thailand, Phim and his men on April 24 rested near Sdau, the village where his wife lived at the end of the war. As they resumed their march, Phim for reasons the refugee did not explain sensed danger and split the party into a group of four, with which he remained, and a group of three. They were to move westward by different routes and rendezvous in the mountains 6 kilometers west of Sdau.

Outside Sdau communist soldiers surrounded Phim and his companions. Apparently, they could have escaped. But as they were well armed, Phim chose to stay and fight to kill as many communists as possible. There ensued a three-hour firefight during which Phim and two others in his party died. Out of the second group, two also were killed by the communists. The two survivors, one from each group, rendezvoused as planned and made their way back to Thailand.

Neither Ponchaud nor the authors can verify this story told by the refugee, who claimed to be one of the survivors. But we find no reason to doubt it.

into a New Village near Chineak. Late in October 1975
Nhek instructed his family to gather in the fields after
dark. Unless they escaped Cambodia, he reasoned, all
would soon starve. Each night in the jungle his
nineteen-year-old son, who was extremely weak and
violently ill from eating pig food, would say, "I pray
that I may reach Thailand and that I may have something to eat." On their tenth day of flight, 15 kilometers from the border, the son died. Two days later
Nhek's brother also died of starvation. In Thailand his
oldest daughter remained hospitalized in critical
condition for months.

Virtually everywhere the jungles reeked of death.
Muslims were especial victims of persecution, and
Abdul Hajji Mohammad, who was one of the few able
to escape, remembers, "We walked for ten nights,
moving only when it was dark. All along the way the
jungle smelled of rotting corpses; at no time could we
get away from that smell."

The jungles also were studded with unforgettable
sights. Ouk Phon, who escaped from Phum To Tea in
the Samrong district, remembers: "No one bothered
to bury the bodies. In one spot I saw about fifty
corpses tied together with rope and elsewhere, under
a tree, the skeleton of a child, its hands still tied. On
the way to the border I suppose I passed more than
five thousand bodies. Some paths were so thick with
skeletons the bones could cut my feet."

In a clearing, Chorn Dayouth, the gem prospector
from Pailin, came upon eleven corpses. Atop the
bullet-torn body of a woman was a two- or three-
year-old child who out of love and fear still was hug-
ging his mother.

Still, they kept coming. One who never gave up was
Ngy Duch, who back in Pailin long ago, it now

seemed, had welcomed peace with melodies from his flute.

When Ngy awoke in the tree where he had taken refuge from the tiger, the beast had gone. But another problem had arisen. Ngy's friend, the soldier Nop Eung, had brooded all night about the perils of escape, remembering the thirty or so inhabitants of Ampil Pram Daum shot while trying to flee.

"Let's go back and tell the Khmer Rouge we got lost in the forest," Nop proposed. "I'm sure nothing will happen to us." Ngy was dumbfounded. His friend was tall, strong and a veteran of jungle combat. And Ngy knew well that the only question about what would happen to them if they returned was how they would be put to death. He rejected the proposal as suicidal and with the aid of two sticks walked off into the jungle. Having no choice, Nop followed.

On the second night of their flight, still apprehensive about tigers, they again climbed a tree and tied themselves to limbs so they could sleep. Ngy prayed to Buddha, "Please ask the tigers to avoid us."

Nop, a professed atheist, laughed and ridiculed the prayer. "Do you really think that will be of any help? I only hope the tigers take orders from your God."

Almost blinded by rain, they had difficulty advancing on the third day until they happened upon a trail marked by fresh footprints made by Ho Chi Minh sandals. "Look what you are getting us into!" Nop angrily exclaimed. "Yesterday you were too afraid to go back because of the Khmer Rouge. Today you are leading us straight to the Khmer Rouge, who will certainly kill us. Why don't you ever listen to me?"

"Shut up!" Ngy ordered. "If you keep quiet, we can hear anyone approaching. On a good track like this, we can cover fifteen kilometers in a day." They continued on the trail until darkness, encountering no one.

Before sleeping, Ngy offered another prayer. "Please keep the Khmer Rouge away from us or, if that is not possible, please seal their eyes so they will not see us."

"Stop this silly praying," Nop interrupted. "You got us into this mess. It's up to you to get us out. Don't rely on your God."

In the morning, their fourth in the jungle, they awoke hungry and without food. "Please send us a good and generous man who will give us something to eat," Ngy prayed. His friend burst into scornful laughter.

They proceeded along the trail without incident until midafternoon, when suddenly they heard rifle shots. "That's the answer to your stupid prayer," Nop whispered. "Your good and generous man is a Khmer Rouge who will kill us both. Hurry, let's get off this murderous trail."

Ignoring him, Ngy hobbled on alone, bending over almost double in an effort to conceal himself. In this fashion he moved slowly for perhaps an hour. Then he abruptly stopped at the sight of a pair of feet in the middle of the trail. On the feet were not Ho Chi Minh sandals but tennis shoes. Ngy stood up and found himself face to face with an armed Thai bandit, who peppered him with questions. "Where do you come from? . . . How many of you are there? . . . Do you have any arms?"

In the midst of the interrogation Nop ran down the trail and, in an obeisance customarily reserved for elderly parents or monks, knelt and lowered his forehead to the ground at the feet of the bandit. Then he uttered a Khmer expression traditionally spoken after a great success or escape from death. "Oh, I am alive! I am alive!"

Another Thai emerged from the brush, and the two thoroughly searched the Cambodians, taking Ngy's jewels and gold and Nop's extra clothes. "Walk along this trail until you see a sign pointing left," the first bandit instructed. "Stop and cry, 'Toot, toot!' Then somebody will feed you."

They did as told, and sure enough, down the trail, when they gave the signal, another bandit appeared with bountiful portions of rice and monkey meat. Ngy and Nop ate three bowls full of each, so much they felt sick. The bandit pointed westward. "You are twenty-two kilometers from Thailand. You will come to a river, and on the other side is Thailand."

As they started out, Ngy said, "You see now that my prayers are being heard."

"Don't be stupid; we were just lucky," said Nop, rushing ahead so fast that Ngy could barely keep up. The next day they waded into the river, and across the water Ngy could see freedom. However, he now was very weak, and toward midstream he slipped and was swept away by the powerful river current. He struggled feebly but vainly against the current, and as his last strength ebbed, he fell back on prayer. Then he felt a strong tug on his belt. Nop had him and towed him to safety and Thailand. A woman directed them to a pagoda a kilometer away. Ngy remembers that as he tried to walk on his swollen leg, the pagoda seemed 100 kilometers away.

After monks ministered to him at the temple, Ngy was taken to the Aranyaprathet refugee camp. "At the camp, the only thing I still had left was my flute. I played it every day, and all the Khmer refugees listened and dreamed of the country they had lost."

IX

THE DARKNESS
SETTLES

By the beginning of 1976 *Angka Loeu*'s domination of Cambodia was beyond challenge. The population, socially atomized and physically enfeebled, was utterly at the mercy of its new masters. The second great migration had been completed, and the New Villages were, in their fashion, functioning. The rice crop, described by the communists as "not a bumper one but sufficient for self-supply," had been harvested. Traditional patterns of life were shattered; the basic institutions of the old society, eliminated. Longtime residents of Vietnamese descent had been expelled, and the land sealed off into a veritable hermit kingdom impervious to foreign influence. Now *Angka Loeu* seemingly could afford to stabilize the country and ameliorate the deathly rigors visited on the population, if only in the interests of efficiency and productivity. But that was not to be.

In October 1975 radio monitors of several nations

picked up a signal of what impended. They inter-
cepted a message to the communist commander in
Sisophon ordering him to prepare for the extermination, after the harvest, of *all* former government soldiers and civil servants, regardless of rank, *and their
families.* Word that another wave of massacres was
being plotted spread among communist soldiers, and
some, perhaps inadvertently, perhaps intentionally,
leaked the secret to the people. Consequently, by the
end of the year, rumors that everyone remotely con-
nected with the Lon Nol government, as well as educated people, were doomed circulated widely in New
Villages all over Cambodia. On December 24 in Phum
Srok, west of Sisophon, a friend told former schoolteacher Chou Try that *Angka Loeu* was about to round
up all former civil servants, teachers, soldiers, village
chiefs, ward chiefs and students. There was truth in
the rumors.

In the late afternoon of January 3 at the village of
Tuk Thla, 5 kilometers outside Sisophon, Khmer
Rouge troops seized Thi Champarith, a former private
in the government army who thought he had hidden
his military past. Thi was bound with red nylon cord,
bundled aboard a Land-Rover and driven to Sisophon.
There he joined about 140 other prisoners in a two-
story concrete building near the town market.

Roughly two-thirds of the captives in the makeshift
prison were former military personnel, mostly enlisted men, and the remaining third were students
and teachers. For four days they sat on the floor, their
legs in irons. There were no toilets in the building,
and they were not allowed outside to relieve themselves. There were no formal charges, no interroga-
tions. However, Thi did overhear Khmer Rouge sol-

diers say that *Angka* had ordered mass arrests and executions of former soldiers, teachers and students in the Sisophon area.

About 9 P.M. the ominous red cords were produced, the arms of forty-eight of the prisoners were tied behind their backs and the men were led aboard a truck, which drove westward out of Sisophon on Highway 5. At the Wat Chamcar Knaur (Jackfruit Orchard Temple), a kilometer away, the truck stopped briefly, and five of the thirteen Khmer Rouge guards dismounted. Then the truck moved slowly toward the forest near the temple with the five soldiers, weapons ready, walking behind.

By this time a young prisoner near Thi had succeeded in unfettering himself. Thi noticed on the tray of the truck near a Khmer Rouge guard a piece of metal, actually part of the truck's front bumper. Desperately he whispered to his fellow prisoner, "Hit the guard with it. It's our only chance." Thi's neighbor struck the guard in the head, and the two jumped from the truck. The communists instantly opened fire but in the darkness could not find their targets, and Thi ran into the woods, losing sight of his companion.

The communists appeared not to press the pursuit, turning instead on the forty-six other prisoners, whom they dragged onto the forest trail. Thi, hiding in dense underbrush, heard machine-gun fire for about an hour. Then he heard the truck driving away. Moving only at night, Thi reached Thailand five days later.

After the government surrender, *Angka Loeu* put a thirty-year-old engineer named You in charge of a bridge repair crew working on the Battambang–Pursat section of Highway 5. The engineer performed his nonpolitical work just as faithfully and competently for the communists as he had done while a civil servant under the Lon Nol government. In January his crew was assigned to a job 30 kilometers southeast of Pailin and required to leave their families in Moung, a village midway between Pailin and Battambang. At the end of January one of You's workers obtained permission to visit his family briefly.

The worker returned with awful news for You. At midnight on February 1 a communist detachment arrested six women, together with their children, and led them from Moung. No explanation was given. The next day a villager looking for sugarcane near the town came across the bodies of the six mothers and their children. Among them were the corpses of You's wife and two small daughters.

When he learned February 3 of the slaughter of his family, the engineer was so overcome that he could not work, and he told his soldier supervisor he was ill. *Angka* sent him to a Battambang hospital, and there a nurse warned, "The Khmer Rouge are planning to kill you. The *Phum Pheak Peayab 1* [Village Battalion Northwest 1] soon will be coming for you." Shortly thereafter soldiers did come and take You away. He was not heard from again.

Rumors that a new pogrom against soldiers, students and the educated impended also swept through Kom Peng, a village southwest of Pursat. And in early January a party of villagers sent northeast to cut wood near Bac Tra village sighted something that made them take the rumors seriously—three large graves gouged out by bulldozers. "There were about sixty or seventy bodies in each grave," remembers Nong Choy Moc Ra, a former schoolteacher. "They had been only partly covered by the bulldozers, and I could see remains of women and children. I don't know exactly how many children. I didn't count them. Looking at the graves made me sick."

Fearful that his name would appear on the latest death lists, Nong and a friend—Ouk Vichet, a former male nurse—sneaked out of Kom Peng on February 6 and headed west toward Thailand's province of Trat. On the fourth day of their flight they stumbled on further evidence that the new massacres were continuing.

Ouk was the first to spot the grave. "Beside the cart track we were following, I saw the remains of a human head, then some bodies half covered with dirt," he said. "Wild animals seemed to have dug up the grave and scattered some of the corpses." The ten or so dead included women and children. Nearby were charred remnants of clothing and personal belongings apparently burned by the executioners. A few kilometers farther on Nong and Ouk saw a horde of flies swarming around another partially open grave. By the end of the day the men had counted six graves big enough to hold more than sixty corpses. The next day, at the foot of a mountain in central Pursat Province, they passed two more graves containing perhaps twenty bodies.

In the early months of 1976 reports of the disappearance or execution of former soldiers, students and educated people were received from numerous other parts of Cambodia. By April the Thai Ministry of the Interior stated that it had gathered positive evidence that the new purges were being carried out in at least nine of the nineteen provinces that existed before the communist conquest: Battambang, Kompong Cham, Kompong Thom, Kampot, Koh Kong, Oddar Meanchey, Pursat, Siem Reap and Thmar Puok.

Executions additionally were reported in areas around Phnom Penh.

However, the odyssey of Dr. Oum Nal, a distinguished Phnom Penh physician, indicates that *Angka Loeu* elected to spare the lives of some intellectuals and even certain military officers, at least for a while. Driven from Preah Net Preah Hospital on April 17, Dr. Oum toiled in rice fields 40 kilometers northwest of Phnom Penh until September 25, when he was caught up in the second great migration. Like Ang Sokthan, he traveled by Chinese truck to Pursat, then by train to Sisophon. There a former male nurse who had joined the Khmer Rouge in 1972 befriended him.

Angka had appointed the ex-nurse "chief doctor" of a Sisophon hospital, and under his patronage Dr. Oum obtained a job washing dishes and sweeping floors at the hospital. The "chief doctor" was a humane man. "Never say no to *Angka*, whatever they ask," he privately counseled his former superior. And once Dr. Oum heard him urge at a Khmer Rouge meeting that medical care be given the malaria-ridden New Villagers being imported into the area. "In some families half the members have died already," he said.

On January 2, 1976, Dr. Oum was taken to the small village of Chup. In a large hangarlike structure near the pagoda were assembled almost 400 "technicians" —skilled workers, professionals, students, intellectuals. Under the direction of a Comrade Sar, they spent several days writing, then rewriting, their biographies for scrutiny by *Angka*.

"One evening we attended a theatrical performance," Dr. Oum recalls. "The Khmer Rouge were singing revolutionary songs and playing revolu-

tionary music. Then there was a short play in which
a Khmer Rouge was insulted, beaten and tortured by
Lon Nol soldiers. The latter wore mustaches and
made terrible grimaces throughout. Some of the
young people burst out laughing. There was an immediate reprimand over the loudspeaker system:
'You are not here to laugh.' "

After writing their biographies a third time, all
physicians, engineers and architects, a total of forty-
five men, were lined up and driven away in a jeep and
two trucks. Just inside Battambang they were stopped
by an *Angka* official holding a sheet of paper in his
hand. "All those whose names are on my list can
return to Phnom Penh," he announced. He then read
the names of three physicians and nine engineers.

"They were deadly white as they climbed out and
entered a brick building guarded by two Khmer
Rouge soldiers. The door closed behind them, and I
don't know what became of them," Dr. Oum remembers.

The remaining thirty-three "technicians" were
locked up in the Central Battambang Prison, which in
the next weeks filled with other intellectuals. "About
two weeks after we came, twenty of the men who had
stayed behind at Chup arrived," says Dr. Oum. "They
had irons around their arms attached with chains that
passed behind their backs. The soldiers took off the
chains in front of us. Under the irons, all had open,
infected, ugly sores. They all gave off the most hor-
rible stench. They told me they had been in prison
at Sisophon, where they had had chains on their
feet also. They couldn't move and had to relieve
themselves where they were, without being able to
take off their clothes. Many of them suffered from

acute dysentery." Shortly afterward *Angka* deposited forty more men in the prison, among them gendarmerie officers, two pilots, a lieutenant colonel, two physicians and an engineer. Next came about 100 students between fourteen and twenty years old.

Angka spokesmen attempted to indoctrinate the prisoners at night, repeatedly sounding a basic refrain: "All of you are technicians. You are educated men, and the simple village people didn't dare reeducate you. But we, your brothers from the army, are happy to have you here, to reeducate and reshape you. In two years' time, maybe, when you have adapted yourselves to the new regime, you will be allowed to return to Phnom Penh and your former profession. Meanwhile, you have to help *Angka* produce rice, to defend the country. Never refuse *Angka*'s orders, and stop thinking about your families."

During the next weeks the prison gradually emptied as *Angka* periodically removed small groups of intellectuals to undisclosed destinations. Dr. Oum had no way of knowing what happened to them. But on March 21 or 22 he and the other thirty-two men with whom he entered prison were transferred to Battambang's Kandal Pagoda, which had been converted into a kind of jail. They stayed at the temple jail more than two weeks during which a sophisticated, cultured communist lectured them about world affairs, emphasizing Cambodia's friendship with China and its plan to base the economy on rice production. Then, on April 6, Dr. Oum and forty-three others were transported by truck to Poy Samrong, a village 21 kilometers to the north.

To Dr. Oum, Poy Samrong seemed like a model

village composed of attractive houses built on stilts. It was well organized, according to military pattern. A group of thirty families formed a regiment, ten families a battalion and ten individuals a platoon. Each platoon had a leader, and the remaining nine members were divided into three groups. Each trio also had a leader, officially called the spy, who was responsible for the other two. Here rice was not doled out daily in a milk tin as elsewhere in Cambodia. Instead, the people ate in communal dining halls, were allowed three or four bowls of rice a day and sometimes enjoyed fish as well. Dr. Oum never found out what *Angka* actually had in store for him and the forty-three other intellectuals settled in Poy Samrong. For on April 17, 1976, the celebrated anniversary of the communist conquest, he slipped away and after a fifteen-day trek entered Thailand.

Perhaps, contrary to the frequent assertions that educated people would not be needed in Democratic Cambodia, *Angka Loeu* had decided that selected intellectuals should be "reshaped" for future use. Perhaps it intended to create in Poy Samrong a "model" village for exhibition purposes. Or maybe in time Dr. Oum and the others would have been liquidated in the same fashion as students and teachers in other villages.

Be that as it may, the experiences of Dr. Oum in Poy Samrong were unique among those of all the refugees interviewed by the authors and their associates. Indeed, the accounts of most refugees fleeing in 1976 emphasized the unrelenting terror, which, if anything, worsened with each passing month. While instituting the new purges, *Angka Loeu* appeared determined to lash "the people of the Emigration" onward toward greater sacrifices, irrespective of the consequences.

François Ponchaud, the noted French authority on Cambodia, reports that on January 26 an *Angka* official in the Mongkol Borei district declared, "To build a democratic Cambodia by renewing everything on a new basis; to do away with every reminder of colonial and imperialist culture, whether visible or tangible or in a person's mind; to rebuild our new Cambodia, one million men is enough. *Prisoners of war [people expelled from the cities and villages controlled by the government on April 17] are no longer needed, and local chiefs are free to dispose of them as they please.*"

The commander of a thirty-man communist detachment stationed at a large farm 8 kilometers west of Sisophon summoned New Villagers and warned: "Everything which belonged to the old society must be banished." All behavior henceforth had to be "revolutionary"; all conversation was to be conducted in "revolutionary terms"; any lapses into "old ways" would be "punished severely."

To exemplify what it expected, *Angka* mounted a propaganda campaign glorifying a teenage girl named Phali. The girl lived in Kandal, a village in the Preah Net Preah district, where whole families continued to perish of famine even after the 1975 harvest. Her father died of starvation and overwork in January, and her mother soon followed him. Leaving her three brothers, who were six, eight, and twelve years old, to fend for themselves in the village, Phali volunteered to work in a distant rice paddy. The boys imitated their late parents by combing the jungle for roots and greenery to eat. Selecting nourishing jungle food

and rejecting the poisonous requires experience,
however. In February all three boys died of something
they had eaten, their limbs grotesquely swollen by
malnutrition. Now *Angka Loeu* heaped even
more public praise on Phali for persevering in revolutionary diligence despite her personal grief. The
propaganda campaign abruptly ended late in
February—after Phali died of malaria.

The first harvest under the communists abated
starvation in many areas of Cambodia. However, distribution problems, exports to Vietnam and insufficient allocations to some settlements caused pockets
of hunger to persist. After the harvest the food supply
improved markedly in the village of Stung Trach in
the Moung Russei district. But according to former
Phnom Penh schoolteacher Song Chin Eth, by February 1976 the village again was beset by an acute rice
shortage, and malnutrition contributed to many
deaths in the spring. Of the 15 members in his family,
Song alone survived, and when he fled in June, only
about 450 of the original 1,000 or so inhabitants of the
village complex were still alive.

Chhrap Chas, a village of 845 inhabitants in the
Preah Net Preah district of Battambang Province, was
more fortunate. Rice stocks there were adequate until
the start of the rainy season in May, when the daily
ration once more was cut to one milk can per person.
During the summer, some thirty people, mostly children, died of starvation; another seventy or so, prin-
cipally older people weakened by malnutrition, succumbed to malaria, dysentery and other diseases.

But rather than alleviate demands on the villagers,
Angka intensified them. Working hours in Chhrap
Chas had been from 6 to 11 A.M. and noon to 6 P.M.

Commencing on August 1, *Angka* required the villagers to work from 3 A.M. to 6 P.M. with an hour respite for lunch. Furthermore, whenever moonlight made cultivation of the fields feasible at night, they were compelled to labor an additional three hours, from 7 to 10 P.M.

Simultaneously, *Angka* identified and proclaimed the existence of a dreaded new malady—*chhoeu sattek aram*, literally, "memory sickness." *Angka* considered that a person was suffering from "memory sickness" if he or she thought too much about life in precommunist Cambodia. The surest symptom of "memory sickness": failure to report for a full day of work.

When a sick individual appealed for respite from labor, soldiers initially were solicitous. "Don't worry," they would say. "If you worry, you'll only get worse. You'll begin thinking about the old days." The implied threat compelled some people to drag themselves back out to the fields for a few more days until they died a squalid death in a rice paddy, in an irrigation ditch or at a dam site. If a person was too incapacitated to work, despite all exertions of will, then after one week *Angka* declared him or her a victim of "memory sickness." *Angka* attempted to cure the ailment by halving the rice ration of the afflicted.

Sometimes the punishment for presumed malingering was more swift and direct. A former Phnom Penh newspaperman, Sou Satra, during the summer of 1976 lived in a large settlement, Unlong Run, west of Battambang. There he knew a seventeen-year-old boy named Sieng Touch. While working in the fields, the boy fainted several times, probably from malnutrition, and soldiers allowed him to rest for three days. Then they abruptly took him away. Reports Sou Satra: "I went with his brother to look for him. We found his body beside a soldiers' hut about 200 meters from the village. He had been disemboweled—there was a deep slash from chest to navel. We saw the bile gland hanging up to dry on the wall of the hut. The Khmer Rouge believed that a useful medicine could be made from the bile duct."

In Chhrap Chas, Unlong Run and elsewhere, *Angka Loeu* also harshened restrictions on courtship and marriage. Flirtation and certainly any physical contact between the unmarried were forbidden, and there was no second chance for violators. A young dam worker named Phan foolishly confided to fellow workers in Chhrap Chas that he had made love to a girl. After they reported him to *Angka*, both he and the girl vanished.

According to Sou Satra, "If someone falls in love in Unlong Run and fails to inform *Angka*, the penalty is death. If you talk to your fiancée's parents ahead of *Angka*, you're killed."

In Pheas, a village east of Thmar Puok town, a former student, Klod Viet, was caught joking and laughing with a teenage girl whom he had known since childhood. "They weren't courting," said Klod's younger brother, who later escaped to Thailand. "She was our cousin." Soldiers accused the youths of planning marriage without the prior sanction of *Angka*. Despite Klod's explanation that their friendliness was born of a long-standing family relationship, the soldiers battered his skull in with ax handles. Then they led the girl into the jungle, and she did not reappear.

Having interviewed recent escapees and analysts in

Bangkok, Washington *Post* correspondent Lewis M. Simons in November 1976 surveyed reports of conditions then prevailing in Cambodia. His dispatch indicates that as 1976 drew to an end, there had been no surcease from the misery and terror. In some areas the daily rice ration was back down to the famine level of 1975—half a can per person. *Angka Loeu* was still ferreting out former soldiers, teachers, monks. Those uncovered still were being led away, their hands bound by red nylon cord, never to be seen again.

No one can possibly know precisely how many people have perished under the terror of *Angka Loeu*. But through analysis of the considerable data now available, it is possible to make a conservative estimate.

One estimate that commands respect comes from Father Ponchaud, who lived in Cambodia from 1965 to 1975. His mission was not to proselytize but to study Buddhism and Cambodia, and he became one of the foremost religious writers in the Khmer language. He has been critical of both American and French policies in Indochina, and his calculations are unlikely to be biased by political considerations. After interviewing a large number of the Cambodian refugees given asylum in France and studying the daily broadcasts of Radio Phnom Penh, Ponchaud concluded that between April 17, 1975, and February 1976, at least 800,000 Cambodians died in consequence of starvation, disease and executions. In the summer of 1976 he spent a month in Thailand eliciting fresh data from refugees who fled subsequent to the new wave of massacres. Given this new information, he concluded that his earlier estimate of 800,000 was "far below reality."

French journalist Yves-Guy Berges in the newspaper *France Soir* in June 1976 stated that he had interviewed hundreds of refugees in Thailand. He wrote that they reported "collective assassinations, reprisals, manhunts after the middle class, massive deportations, forced labor, disappearance, death, always death, familiar, omnipresent, to the point of nausea." Concluded Berges: "In these conditions, the figure of a million victims since April 17, 1975, the day of the 'liberation' of Phnom Penh, is plausible, if not certain."

Khieu Samphan, as Cambodian chief of state, attended the Colombo Conference of nonaligned nations in August 1976 and while there was interviewed by the Italian weekly magazine *Famiglia Cristiana.* "Those traitors that remained have been executed," the magazine quoted him as saying. It further quoted him: "In five years of warfare, more than one million Cambodians died. The current population of Cambodia is five million. Before the war, the population numbered seven million."*

The interviewer asked, "If one million persons died in the fighting, what happened to the remaining one million?"

"It's incredible how concerned you Westerners are about war criminals," the magazine quoted him as replying.

*Referring to the war toll, Khieu Samphan in his public address at the Colombo Conference stated: "More than one million people out of a population of eight million were killed. . . ."

So far as the authors can ascertain, no one heretofore had contended that the prewar population of Cambodia was much more than seven million, and we can find no basis for believing it was higher. As indicated earlier, neither have we been able to find any reliable basis on which to compute the number of war fatalities with any certainty.

Thus, if quoted accurately, Khieu Samphan indicated that between April 17, 1975, and the time of the interview in August 1976 roughly a million Cambodians died.

The authors, on the basis of their own data, calculate that the number of deaths inflicted by *Angka Loeu* between April 17, 1975, and the end of 1976 is even higher.

On April 18, 1975, the day after the evacuation began, Fernand Scheller, chief of the United Nations development project in Phnom Penh, declared, "What the Khmer Rouge are doing is pure genocide. They will kill more people this way than if there had been fighting in the city. There is no food outside. The next rice crop is not until December. . . . What is going on now is an example of demogoguery that makes one vomit."

Western observers in Phnom Penh, including at least one French physician, who saw the masses forced out of the city during those first days estimated that more than 200,000 of them would die. But because they could not anticipate the duration of the march, the terrible circumstances in which it was enforced and the hostility of the environment where survivors settled, their estimate surely is too low. Considering the testimony of all the survivors interviewed, together with all other available data, we estimate that of the 4,000,000 driven from the cities and government-controlled villages, a minimum of 10 percent, or 400,000, succumbed.

The approximately 3,600,000 survivors of the march bore the brunt of the famine that began in June and continued throughout the year. Its effects were magnified by the second great migration that again displaced half a million people in the fall. Refugees who escaped in late August and September all reported high numbers of deaths from starvation and disease in their areas. According to their accounts, *during the summer alone* 5 percent of the original population of some New Villages died of disease and starvation, and in others, up to 30 percent perished. Refugees who fled later in the year generally reported even higher tolls. All spoke of high percentages of people who were too weak to walk or stand upright. Considering the lack of medical treatment and that the benefits of the harvest could not be realized until late in the year, a goodly proportion of the moribund must have died. Therefore, we conservatively conclude that at least 12 percent of the 3,600,000 survivors of the Emigration—some 430,000—died of starvation and disease during 1975.

The harvest reaped in December 1975 appears to have abated the acute malnutrition in much of Cambodia, at least during the first half of 1976. But the effects of the tropical squalor to which "people of the Emigration" were consigned, the absence of medicine, the slaughter of doctors, the inadequacy of herbal medicine, the ineptitude of communist medical orderlies and the grueling work regimen did not abate during 1976. Indeed, communist statements suggest that the problems of disease worsened in 1976, and their effects on the mortality rate probably offset considerably the benefits of an increased food supply. Moreover, there were indications that by autumn of 1976 famine again stalked sections of the country just as it did during the same period of the preceding year. Thus, we have no reason to believe that the rate of death from disease and malnutrition in the New Villages during the last six months in 1976 was substantially lower than after completion of the exodus in 1975. But if we assume that it was only 8 percent, or two-thirds as high, we find that more than 250,000 of the 3,200,000 evacuees presumed to have survived 1975 died during 1976.

Although the authorized strength of the government army at the end of the war was 230,000, U.S. military and State Department sources believe Lon Nol military personnel did not number more than 200,000. There were an estimated 30,000 civil servants and 20,000 teachers. The number of "educated people" and students marked for extermination cannot be determined. So for purposes of calculation, we will assume that approximately 250,000 people, not counting their families, were targets of the massacres ordered in 1975 and 1976. Overwhelming evidence shows that in all parts of the land they have been hunted down pervasively, continuously and relentlessly. If we assume that 20 percent of them died of hunger or disease and that *Angka Loeu* has managed to detect and kill only half of the remaining 80 percent, we still find that approximately 100,000 former military personnel, civil servants and teachers have been executed.

We lack sufficient data to estimate reasonably the number of women and children executed because they were related to military personnel or civil servants. Similarly, there is no way of knowing how many New Villagers were executed not because of their background but merely because they displeased *Angka*.

It also is difficult to calculate the number of Cambodians who died attempting to flee the country through the forests and jungles, but here a conservative estimate is possible. The Thai Ministry of the Interior advised the authors that as of November 1976, 11,086 refugees had registered with the government. It estimated that roughly an equal number had entered and were living in Thailand illegally, without having registered. Refugee accounts clearly indicate that of all who attempted to escape, fewer than half succeeded. So it seems reasonable to assume that at least 20,000 died trying to flee.

Therefore, we conclude that at the very minimum, more than 1,200,000 men, women and children died in Cambodia between April 17, 1975, and January 1, 1977, as a consequence of the actions of *Angka Loeu*: 400,000 or more during the first exodus; 430,000 or more from disease and starvation during the latter half of 1975; 250,000 or more from disease and starvation in 1976; 100,000 or more in massacres and by execution; and 20,000 or more during escape attempts.*

What have these deaths and the incalculable pain, anguish, horror and suffering that accompanied them brought to pass?

Let us listen to *Angka Loeu*. On July 20, 1976, Pol Pot, then premier of Democratic Cambodia, granted an interview to Tran Thanh Xuan, deputy editor in

---

*Paucity of data precludes consideration of the effects all the convulsions have had upon the estimated 3,000,000 Cambodians living in territory controlled by the Khmer Rouge at the end of the war. Conditions of life in these areas doubtless were better by far than in the New Villages, and the inhabitants were not weakened by the rigors of the exodus. However, evacuees from the cities may have spread epidemics and thereby increased the mortality rate in these areas.

chief of the Vietnam News Agency. Cambodian Foreign Minister Ieng Sary, another of the original masters of *Angka Loeu,* was present. The text of the interview subsequently was broadcast in English by Radio
Hanoi.

"Would you please tell us about the achievements
recorded by the Cambodian people in various aspects
after the total liberation?" the interviewer asked.

In a rambling reply Pol said:

"On the social welfare aspect, we have paid attention to the eradication of malaria. We learned that so
far over eighty percent of our labor force was
exhausted by malaria. Many times in the harvest season, the people were stricken with malaria and became too weak to work. We have built many hospitals,
dispensaries and trained many medical cadres during
the war as well as in peace, but the knowledge of our
cadres is still low. At present, dispensaries have been
set up at each cooperative, but the weak point is that
the medical knowledge of cadres is still low, and we
do not have sufficient medicines. Our traditional
medicines are abundant, but the effects are not high.
The import of foreign medicines has been limited.
However, we have made a step forward in the social
and medical fields as compared with the prewar time
and 1975.

"In short, we have not made any noteworthy
achievements except the revolutionary movement of
the masses. Through this movement, we have
achieved preliminary results and made progress as
compared with last year, but we have to make more
efforts to meet the ever-rising needs and requirements
of the people. We only have our bare hands after the
war. Therefore, we have to strive hard, and our

achievements scored so far are only initial ones. We believe that our situation will more finely develop thanks to the seething revolutionary movement of the masses. We are sure that we will make progress because our revolution relies on the people, and the people have had such a seething movement."*

After the destruction of more than 1,000,000 human beings, a once happy country and a whole civilization, the premier of Democratic Cambodia sums up the accomplishments of *Angka Loeu: In short, we have not made any noteworthy achievements except the revolutionary movement of the masses.*

As Pol Pot indicated in the interview, Cambodia today is a land without universities. It also is a land without cities, commerce, art, music, literature, science or hope. And as the young refugee said, "There is no love anywhere."

Each day *Angka Loeu* speaks to the people through the broadcasts of Radio Phnom Penh. Against a background of revolutionary music, it told them early in 1976, "In the past, in the days of Lon Nol, the arch-traitor, the overcorrupted, the highly harmful, and of his clique, the stooges of the Americans, you were poor and oppressed. You could never enjoy life because you suffered from poverty and hunger. Now, under the enlightened and intelligent leadership of the revolutionary *Angka,* you live in happiness and prosperity."

In the autumn of 1976 *Angka Loeu* broadcast a song

---

*Radio Phnom Penh on September 27, 1976, announced that "for health reasons" Pol Pot had been "suspended" from his post as premier.

whose words perhaps more accurately reflect the life of the surviving Cambodians.

> We took the jungle as our home,
>> Sunlight never reached us; only mosquitoes and land leeches,
> Weak with malaria, we are tree vines,
>> All bones and white, but our hearts were still bright red.

After the desolation of the cities, the early massacres and in midst of the first famine, one of the *Angka Loeu* leaders, Ieng Sary, in his incarnation as foreign minister, flew to a special session of the United Nations General Assembly. Upon landing in New York, he boasted, "We have cleansed the cities," and when he appeared at the United Nations, delegates from around the world warmly applauded.

Otherwise, the world largely has remained almost as silent as the ghostly, decaying remains of the abandoned Cambodian cities. No outraged students protest on campuses. No one demonstrates on Pennsylvania Avenue, the Champs-Élysées or Trafalgar Square about what peace has brought to Cambodia. There is no great outcry in Congress against "corruption" in the new Cambodia.

And in the thousands of New Villages, the Cambodians about whom nobody cares each evening under the guns of *Angka Loeu* try to sleep, knowing that the next day will be as dark as the night that has enveloped them.

ACKNOWLEDGMENTS

Numerous individuals of different nationalities assisted the authors in preparation of this book, and we wish gratefully to acknowledge the contributions of those whom we are at liberty to identify.

Swangchit Indrabhitabse served as our interpreter, making many excursions into remote refugee camps, where she worked under adverse circumstances. Throughout, she inspired by her loyalty, valor, competence and good humor.

Saner Khettasiri of the Thai Ministry of the Interior, out of personal conviction that the world should know what has happened in Cambodia, enabled us to visit a number of refugee camps which otherwise would have been inaccessible. His knowledge and advice additionally provided us with invaluable guidance.

Satienreak "Mike" Thada, chief driver at Bangkok's Oriental Hotel, proved to be something considerably more than a chauffeur. His formidable knowledge of grass-roots Thailand made it possible for us to reach obscure places in the shortest time. His ready charm and wit eased our dealings with rural officialdom.

Hajji Omar Lim, executive secretary of PERKIM, the Muslim Welfare Association in Kuala Lumpur, kindly arranged for access to Malaysia's Cambodian refugee camps.

François Ponchaud put at our disposal his immense store of knowledge about Cambodia, generously shared with us the results of his own research, saved us from errors through scholarly criticism and on several occasions assisted Ursula Naccache as an interpreter in the conduct of important interviews.

Andrew Antippas and T. M. Carney of the U.S. Department of State, Kenneth Quinn of the National Security Council and Colonel Robert Drudik of the U.S. Army General Staff, all of whom have extensive backgrounds in Cambodian affairs, made available large quantities of their own data, guided us to other sources, answered innumerable questions and favored us with authoritative criticism.

Kem Sos, a Cambodian language instructor at the Foreign Service Institute, Department of State, since 1969, provided invaluable assistance in transcribing tapes and locating refugees in the United States.

Patricia Lawson of the Washington bureau of the *Reader's Digest* expertly processed and corrected the manuscript through a number of revisions, guarded against distractions and interruptions during the writing.

Nathan Adams, a senior *Digest* editor, volunteered to interrupt his vacation to scrutinize the manuscript and offered numerous criticisms resulting in its improvement.

William Schulz, chief of the Washington bureau of the *Digest*, out of personal friendship criticized each chapter, provided wise counsel regarding both the research and writing, placed at our disposal all the resources of his bureau and lent constant encouragement.

Kenneth Gilmore, the editor of the book, led and inspired us through each stage of its preparation. From the outset, he acted as both a critical and creative editor, identifying defects and conceiving ideas for their correction. His editing greatly enhanced the final manuscript, which never would have come into being had it not been for his original vision.

CHAPTER NOTES

CHAPTER I

•Phnom Penh prostrate before communists and people sense war is over: Interviews with Father François Ponchaud, architect Ly Bun Heng, librarian Ea Than, Dr. Vann Hay, students Pisot Mao, Ang Sokthan, Yem Rithipol, counselor Heng Huong Khang, teacher Yen Savannary, American businessman Douglas Sapper; New York *Times,* April 17, 18, 1975; Bangkok *Post,* April 18, 1975; *Newsweek,* April 28, 1975.

•Three million people in Phnom Penh: *Far Eastern Economic Review Asia Year Book* (1976), p. 133; *Sunday Times* (London), October 12, 1975 (William Shawcross interview in Paris with Prince Sihanouk); Indochina Resource Center, Washington, D.C., text of remarks by Ieng Sary concerning evacuation of Cambodia's cities and the Mayaguez incident, New York City, September 6, 1975.

•Communist siege of Phnom Penh and use of rockets: Interviews with Ponchaud; Timothy Carney, country officer for Cambodia, U.S. Department of State; Colonel Robert Drudik, General Staff, U.S. Army; Robert Keeley, former deputy chief of mission, U.S. embassy, Phnom Penh; telegram from U.S. Ambassador John

Gunther Dean to secretary of state, February 4, 1974; eyewitness observations of Anthony Paul.

•Populace reception of communists and general relief at war's end: Interviews with Sapper, gendarme Kuy Hong Taing, students Sar Sam, Ung Sok Choeu, Pisot Mao, Norodom Vorapongs (member of Cambodian royal family), Ponchaud, pharmacist Kyheng Savang, Catholic Relief Service worker Pin-Sam Phon, police superintendent Ho Mey, Pech Kim Eng, intelligence officer Thiounn Kamel; New York Times, April 17, May 9, 1975.

•Paucity of popular support for communists: Kenneth M. Quinn, "Political Change in Wartime: The Khmer Krahom Revolution in Southern Cambodia, 1970–1974," presented at American Political Science Association Convention at the San Francisco Hilton on September 4, 1975; Washington Star, April 10, 1974; Christian Science Monitor, March 15, 1974, and January 6, 1975; Chicago Tribune, July 14, 1974; Washington Post, November 24, 1974, and March 3, 1975; Xat Lao (Vientiane) August 9, 1974; New York Times, April 17, 1975; Donald Whitaker, et al., Area Handbook for the Khmer Republic (Cambodia) prepared by the Foreign Area Studies of the American University, Washington, published by U.S. Government Printing Office, 1973 (henceforth referred to as Area Handbook); T. M. Carney, Communist Party Power in Kampuchea (Cambodia): Documents and Discussion, Cornell University Southeast Asia Program Data Paper, forthcoming (henceforth referred to as Carney Paper); interview with Andrew Antippas, former country officer for Cambodia, Department of State.

•By spring 1975 cities had absorbed half of national population: Area Handbook; New York Times, April 17, 1975.

•Corruption of Lon Nol government: New York Times, February 20, August 8, 1974, and March 16, 1975; Christian Science Monitor, March 8, 1974; Sheldon W. Simon, War and Politics in Cambodia (Durham, N.C.: Duke University Press, 1974); Washington Post, February 24, 1974; Far Eastern Economic Review, July 1, 1972; New York Times, May 4, 1975; Los Angeles Times, May 8, 1975; testimony of Ambassador John Gunther Dean, Hearing Before the Special Subcommittee on Investigations of the Committee on International Relations, House, May 5, 1976 (henceforth cited as Dean testimony).

•War caused 600,000 deaths: New York Times, September 8,

1974; *Sunday Times* (London), May 11, 1975; *Le Monde* (Paris), February 17, 18, 1976; *New York Review of Books*, March 4, 1976; *Sunday Telegraph* (London), September 15, 1976.

•Cambodia before the war: *National Geographic*, September 1952, April 1960; interviews with Miss So San, former director of Language Institute, University of Phnom Penh; Pisot Mao; Kem Sos, U.S. Foreign Service Institute instructor, and Mrs. Kem Sos; Counselor Gaffar Peang Meth, former Cambodian embassy, Washington; *New York Review of Books*, March 4, 1976; *Area Handbook*.

•Popular belief that conquerors would be reasonable and just: Interviews with Ung Sok Choeu, banker Siv Hav, Kyheng Savang, Pin Sam Phon and gem prospector Ngy Duch.

•Looting by government forces: Interviews with Ea Than, Ho Mey, and students Thach Bun Rath, Ang Sokthan.

•Government soldiers quickly surrendered weapons: Interviews with Ea Than, Ly Bun Heng, Thiounn Kamel, Ponchaud.

•Behavior of communist soldiers: Interviews with Ly Bun Heng, Ea Than, Ang Sokthan, Ho Mey, Thiounn Kamel, gendarme Thach Ngy, Ponchaud, Kyheng Savang, Pech Kim Eng; Agence France Presse (AFP) report, May 8, 1975; *Sunday Times* (London) May 8, 1975.

•The killings begin: Interviews with Ea Than, Sar Sam, Ho Mey, student Prach Chhea, Thiounn Kamel, Ly Bun Heng, teacher Yen Savannary, medical student Kem Phaly, Kyheng Savang, Heng Huong Kheng; *Sunday Times* (London), May 8, 1975; *Mirror* (London), May 9, 1975, AP dispatch from Bangkok, May 8, 1975.

•Evacuation of Phnom Penh: Interviews with Ponchaud, medical students Ku Soy Try and Kem Phaly, Yen Savannary, Pisot Mao, Sar Sam, Ang Sokthan, Heng Huong Kheng, Ea Than, Pech Kim Eng, student Cham Kanya, law student Vong Khemarak, Kyheng Savang, Professor Phal Oudam, Thiounn Kamel, Yem Rithipol, student Kim Vann Svaing, Captain Ly Sam Poan, Captain Savoeun Tan, philosophy student Thach Bun Roe On, Lieutenants Iem Ly Nuthy and Iem Tim Ravy; *New York Times*, April 19, May 9, 1975; *Sunday Times* (London) May 11, 1975.

•Emptying hospitals of sick and wounded: Interviews with Dr. Vann Hay, Ponchaud, Kem Phaly, Ang Sokthan, Ea Than, Prach Chhea, Drs. Murray Carmichael and Michael Daly and nurse Helen Frazer, members of British medical team at Preah Ket

Melea Hospital, Phnom Penh; New York *Times* April 19, May 9, 1975; *Daily Telegraph* (London), May 7, 1975.

•Destruction of books and printed matter: Interviews with Ly Bun Heng, teacher Nhem Sary, Kem Phaly, Yem Rithipol, Pisot Mao, Ly Sam Poan, Savoeun Tan, former Khmer Rouge soldier Phal So Vichet; New York *Times*, July 15, 1975.

•Radio announcement of surrender and communist statement that they would not negotiate: Interview with former president of the Supreme Committee of the Khmer Republic, Sak Sutsakhan; interview with Timothy Carney; U.S. Foreign Broadcast Information Service Daily Report No. 41, April 17, 1975, citing Radio Phnom Penh broadcasts (henceforth noted as FBIS).

•Suffering of populace during exodus from Phnom Penh: Interviews with Ang Sokthan, Vann Hay, businessman Dost Mohammed, Ly Bun Heng, Tevi Rosa, Vong Khemarak, Ponchaud, Thach Bun Rath, Ea Than, Ho Mey.

•Exodus from other cities: Interviews with Pin Sam Phon, businessman Chheng Savan, Kuy Hong Taing, teacher Sokh Kim Vang, truck driver Ma Chheang, student Nuom Linna, gem salesman Chorn Dayouth, Sergeant Major Sem Vann, Ngy Duch, businessman Hajji Abdul Rahman Samium, Lieutenant Hong Sun Huor, monk Bo Penh.

•Communist boasts that they are turning cities into countryside and countryside into cities: Interview with Siv Hav.

•Hospital massacres at Siem Reap: Interview with Hong Sun Huor, who witnessed the atrocities.

•Transformation of Phnom Penh into a wasteland: Interviews with Ly Bun Heng, Ly Sam Poan, Savoeun Tan, Phal Oudam, Sokh Kim Vang, Yen Savannary; *Daily Telegraph* (London), May 7, 1975; Jean Jacques Cazeaux (AFP), Hong Kong, May 8, 1975; New York *Times* editorial July 9, 1975; New York *Times*, July 15, 1975 (Henry Kamm); Los Angeles *Times*, August 12, 1975; Bangkok *Post*, August 31, 1975; *Sunday Times* (London), October 12, 1975 (William Shawcross interview with Prince Sihanouk); New York *Times*, October 13, 1975 (AFP report from Peking); *France Soir*, October 15, 1975; *Far Eastern Economic Review*, October 24, 1975; Washington *Post*, February 2, 1976; *Time*, April 19, 1976; Washington *Post*, May 4, 1976 (report of defector Lieutenant Pech Lim Kuon).

CHAPTER II

•Khayyám quote is from *Rubaiyát of Omar Khayyám*, rendered into English by Edward Fitzgerald, with illustrations by Edmund Dulac (New York: George H. Doran Co.,).

•Eradication of traditional patterns of life: Interviews with Pisot Mao, Ly Bun Heng, Ponchaud, Dr. Vann Hay, Ea Than, Thiounn Kamel, Ang Sokthan, Ho Mey, Phal Oudam, Yem Rithipol, Nhem Sary, Kem Phaly, border guard Ith Thaim; *Guardian* (Manchester), February 16, 1976; former Khmer Rouge soldier Danh Sang.

•Burning of books and documents: Interviews with Nhem Sary, Kem Phaly, Cham Kanya, Ith Thaim, immigration officer Os Hoeung, Siv Hav, Ly Sam Poan, Savoeun Tan, Iem Ly Vuthy, Iem Tim Revy, Yem Rithipol, Ang Sokthan, Prach Chhea.

•*Angka Loeu* proclaimed birth of the new Cambodia: Radio Phnom Penh domestic service monitored in Bangkok, January 7, 1976 (FBIS).

•The handful of theorists who began *Angka Loeu:* Wilfred Burchett, *Second Indochina War* (New York: International Publishers, 1970); Ith Sarin, *Nine Months with the Maquis* (translated by Department of State, U.S. embassy, Phnom Penh) and *Regrets for the Khmer Soul* (translated by T. M. Carney), 1973; New York Times, April 8, 1975 (Iver Petersen); New York Times, April 17, 1975 (Joseph Treaster); *Le Courrier du Viet Nam* (Hanoi), No. 358, January 31, 1972; *Far Eastern Economic Review*, June 25, 1976 (Edith Lenart); interview with Ieng Sary in *Le Monde* (Paris), January 15, 1972, by Claude Julien; Washington *Post*, March 10, 1974 (Elizabeth Becker); *China Pictorial* (Peking) Supplement to No. 6, 1973; Carney Paper.

•Khieu Samphan as a leading theorist: Ith Sarin, *Nine Months with the Maquis*; Khieu Samphan, *Doctoral Dissertation*, University of Paris, 1959 (translated by U.S. Department of State).

•Life of Khieu Samphan: Interviews with Sen Dikhayuko, former press counselor, Cambodian embassy, Washington; Jack Pavoni, Intelligence and Research Department, Department of State; Pisot Mao; New York Times, April 18, 1975; William Shawcross, *New York Review of Books*, March 4, 1976; *Le Courrier du Viet Nam* (Hanoi), No. 358, January 31, 1972; interviews with classmates in Paris.

•The three Phantoms (Khieu Samphan, Hou Yuon and Hu Nim) go underground: Ith Sarin, *Nine Months with the Maquis* and *Regrets for the Khmer Soul;* Kenneth M. Quinn Airgram to Department of State, February 20, 1974; *Area Handbook.*

•Small size of insurgency forces: *Area Handbook; Orbis,* "The Role of Outsiders in the Cambodian Conflict" by Sheldon W. Simon; Washington *Post,* March 10, 1974 (Becker); Ith Sarin, *Nine Months with the Maquis;* J. L. S. Girling, "The Resistance in Cambodia." *Asian Survey,* 12, No. 7 (July 1972), speaks of a force of between 1,500 and 3,000 men.

•Sihanouk's collaboration with the Vietnamese: *Area Handbook;* New York *Times,* April 17, 1975 (Wolfgang Saxon); *Livre Blanc sur l'Agression Vietcong et Nord-Vietnamienne Contre la République Khmere* (1970–71), edité par le Ministère de l'Information, Phnom Penh.

•Sihanouk becomes exasperated with the Vietnamese: On October 9, 1969, Sihanouk, speaking to students returned from abroad, said "Vietnamese Reds" had already occupied a large part of Ratangkiri Province and were to be found in Prey Veng, Kratie, Svay Rieng and Kompong Cham. (*Chronology of Developments Affecting Cambodia,* U.S. embassy, Phnom Penh, February 1975 [mimeographed], henceforth cited as *Chronology*).

•Sihanouk orders Army Chief of Staff Lon Nol to form a government of national salvation: December 5, 1968, Prime Minister Penn Nouth left for medical care in France, and Lon Nol became acting prime minister. April 26, 1969, Sihanouk said that "to deal with the Vietcong and Vietminh," he had ordered Lon Nol to give up the "defensive spirit" and adopt "offensive spirit." July 31, at opening of the 27th National Congress, Sihanouk said he would accept the resignation of Prime Minister Penn Nouth because of poor health. August 6, announcement was made that General Lon Nol would accept position of prime minister after having initially declined. August 12, a government of National Salvation (*sauvetage*) under Lon Nol was approved by the National Assembly and installed. On September 22, in a special message to the nation issued from his hospital bed, Sihanouk said, ". . . I found Lon Nol the only person I could trust because of his faithfulness to the Throne and Nation . . ." (*Chronology*).

•Deposition of Sihanouk: January 6, 1970, Sihanouk, saying he suffered from "obesity, blood disease and albuminuria," departed

Cambodia for medical treatment abroad. February 18, General Lon Nol, who had himself been abroad for medical treatment, returned to Phnom Penh. March 8, villagers in Svay Rieng Province carried out an anti-Vietnamese demonstration. March 11, Phnom Penh demonstrators sacked the Vietnamese and Vietcong embassies, and Sihanouk announced he would return and demand a referendum so people could choose between him and those who aimed to destroy "friendship between Cambodia and the socialist bloc." But on that same day the National Assembly and Council of the Kingdom passed a resolution supporting the demonstrators. The cabinet also issued an appeal terming acts of demonstrators "worthy of praise." March 13, Sihanouk arrived in Moscow and from there on March 17 sent a message to the queen mother telling of "socialist camp" reactions to developments in Cambodia and of Soviet warning that "low blows" of "extreme right against our allies" could "inevitably mean war between Cambodia and Vietnam."

March 18, joint session of National Assembly and Council of the Kingdom passed a unanimous (92–0) vote of no confidence in Sihanouk. (Soviet Premier Kosygin personally advised Sihanouk of what happened.) The National Assembly then declared a state of "national danger," and constitutional rights were suspended in accordance with Article 15 of the constitution. The airports at Phnom Penh and Siem Reap were closed, and international cable traffic was cut.

March 19, Sihanouk arrived in Peking on a special Aeroflot flight. March 21, Sihanouk renounced what he called the "absurd title of Chief of State" (Chronology); Kansas City Times, April 29, 1975 (William F. Buckley, Jr.); Sihanouk, My War with the CIA, as related to Wilfred Burchett (New York: Pantheon Books, 1972).

•Formation of exile government in Peking: April 10, 1970, Radio Hanoi broadcast statement of support for Sihanouk from Khieu Samphan, Hu Nim and Hou Yuon; April 21, first "Cambodian United Front" appeal was broadcast on the NLF (communist) clandestine radio; May 5, Sihanouk made public the political program of the National United Front of Kampuchea (FUNK) and the composition of the "Royal Government of National Union" which, he said, had been approved at a FUNK congress held in Peking, May 3. The three Phantoms, Khieu Samphan, Hu Nim and Hou Yuon, were declared part of the government. People's Republic of China, Albania, Cuba and Syria promptly recognized the newly formed government.

May 10, Sihanouk's FUNK government formally broke relations with the United States. May 11, Sihanouk told a meeting of various ambassadors in Peking that Khieu Samphan, Hu Nim and Hou Yuon were "in their home country leading the Cambodian people to carry out heroic struggles" (*Chronology*); Donald Kirk, *Wider War: The Struggle for Cambodia, Thailand and Laos* (New York: Praeger, 1971); Sihanouk, *My War with the CIA.*

•North Vietnamese forces in name of Sihanouk attacked Lon Nol forces shortly after formation of coalition: Early in the morning of March 29, 1970, elements of the 5th and 7th North Vietnamese, Vietcong divisions and a Vietnamese artillery group in the sanctuaries north of Tay Ninh Province in South Vietnam began attacks on Cambodian police and army posts. Elements of the 9th Vietcong Division at the same time started moving out of their sanctuary areas in the Mekong-Bassac rivers corridor in the border area and by the middle of April were fighting at the town of Saang some 20 kilometers south of Phnom Penh. The North Vietnamese army moved fast and a month before the American invasion had driven 300 kilometers northwest to the Siem Reap area. These NVA/VC forces were augmented by a unit formed by the Vietnamese from among the thousands of Vietnamese who had lived for years around the Great Lake of Cambodia: Andrew Antippas; Albert M. Burger, Naval War College; Dean testimony.

•American and South Vietnamese divisions invaded Cambodia. The American role in this limited incursion lasted sixty days and succeeded militarily: Kirk, *op. cit.*

•Americans pull out, communists in control of larger areas than before and arrival of Cambodian communists trained in North Vietnam: *Orbis, op. cit.,* p. 211; the North Vietnamese army had since 1954 trained a cadre and prepared to begin a revolutionary war at such time as the removal of Sihanouk suited their purposes. This cadre was put on the trail within weeks of Sihanouk's ouster and under cover of the Vietnamese army, which slashed deep into Cambodia (Antippas); in his paper, Carney reports that the number of Cambodians who went north in 1954 varies from 2,500 to 4,000 men and that the North Vietnamese told Sihanouk that 8,000 Cambodians had gone south to support his return (to power). Carney stated that his information came from Ker

Chhieng, a member of Sihanouk's private office who defected to Phnom Penh in January 1973 and described his travels with Sihanouk to Hanoi at a January 29, 1973, press conference which Carney attended. Carney further reported that the difference in figures may reflect additional men who continually filtered north during Sihanouk's rule.

•People begin flight to cities: Dean testimony; at least 28,000 people fled from southern Cambodia alone into South Vietnam and an estimated 20,000 to 25,000 others to Khmer government-controlled areas, according to USAID figures for 1973 quoted by Quinn; Quinn also reports that 45,000 people fled a communist-controlled area; Ieng Sary, foreign minister of the new Democratic Cambodia, said in New York in September, 1975, that his government had found an unexpected 3,000,000 people in Phnom Penh.

•Communists gain control of coalition but keep Sihanouk as figurehead for international scrutiny: Washington *Post,* March 10, 1974 (Elizabeth Becker); "Late 1971 to early 1973 the communists broke away from domination by the North Vietnamese, gained control of FUNK, dropped its allegiance to Sihanouk, purged the cadre and then began their program to radically change Cambodian society." At the local level they dropped the term "royal" (*reach*) from the name of their government and replaced it with *kana* (which means sect, party or committee), making the new title of the government in areas under their control Kana Rothaphibal Ronasey Ruoprumchet Kampuchea or the Party Government of the United National Front. However, they did not make such a change in name at the national or international level. Therefore, references to the "royal" government continued, and Sihanouk continued to be acknowledged as "chief of state" (Quinn, *Political Change in Wartime*); Ith Sarin's *Regrets for the Khmer Soul;* Donald Kirk, "The Khmer Rouge: Revolutionaries or Terrorists," presented at SEADAG Ad Hoc Seminar on Communist Movements and Regimes in Indochina, September 30, 1974; law student Vong Khemarak told the editors that the communists called Sihanouk *A Kanthort, A Kampsung, A Kantoeur,* or "Mr. Fat, Mr. Big Stomach, Mr. Short."

•Prince Sihanouk realized what was happening: AFP report from Peking, September 26, 1970; Oriana Fallaci's June 23, 1972, interview with the prince as printed in the New York *Times,* August 12, 1973.

•Sihanouk continued to front for communists: Roger Kershaw's evaluation was published in *The World Today*, February 1976.

•Myth of three factions in communist leadership: Washington *Post*, March 10, 1974 (Becker).

•Communists make every effort to preserve Sihanouk myth: *Far Eastern Economic Review*, October 24, 1975; declaration of front's objectives published in Paris which, in addition to promises quoted, said that Buddhism would remain the state religion.

•Sihanouk and entourage returned to Cambodia and were unable to find old friends: New York *Times*, October 18, 1975; *Far Eastern Economic Review*, October 24, 1975.

•Communists rarely refer to themselves as such but speak of *Angka*: Ith Sarin, *Regrets for the Khmer Soul*; earliest broadcast use of term *Angka* was made March 1971, according to Carney Paper.

•North Vietnamese withdraw their troops: January 28, 1973, Lon Nol ordered unilateral suspension of military offensive operations pending North Vietnamese and Vietcong withdrawal from Cambodia. This came one day after the peace accords on Vietnam were signed in Paris, Article 20 of which required withdrawal of all foreign troops from Cambodia (*Chronology*).

•Khieu Samphan and colleagues in control of enlarged insurgency force: Orbis, *op. cit.*, p. 209; Ith Sarin reported that the party ensured control by assigning a party political commissar (*Snong Kar*) to monitor the activities of the entire committee for the village, district and sector, thus indicating the key role these intermediate units must have played in production, military recruitment and population control (Carney Paper).

CHAPTER III

•Surrender of the Battambang garrison: Interviews with Sem Vann and Thach Ngy.

•Sihanouk's March 20 pledge of no bloodbath: FBIS, March 20, 1975.

•Execution of Dr. Tan Pok: Interviews with Thach Ngy and Young Phorn.

•Massacre at Mount Tippadei: Interviews with three survivors, Majors Phim Uon, Kom Kiry and Ouk Phansy Kamphon. Corroborating details were provided by Sem Vann, Thach Ngy, Young Phorn, Nuom Linna, Siv Hav, Yen Savannary, Lieutenant Tok Saream, Sergeant Nay Chea Sarunsarak; Khmer Rouge medical orderly Keo Su Wan; *Newsweek*, May 12, 1975.

•Communists set out to exterminate high-ranking government military and civil service officers: Interviews with Ponchaud, Vann Hay, Kyheng Savang, Kem Phaly, Sergeant Seng Lmouth *Daily Telegraph* (London), April 8, 1976.

•Massacre at Mongkol Borei: Interviews with Ith Thaim, merchant Chhun Sun, Corporal Keo Kim Taun, farmer Sam Oeun, Sergeant Cheap Boeun; *Le Figaro* (Paris) October 10, 1975.

•Ambush of the Sisophon government officers: Interviews with Kim Sath and former Khmer Rouge soldier Penh Choerm.

•Clubbing to death of seventeen officers from Preah Net Preah who had been told they were being taken to Angkor Wat: Interview with Lieutenant Nuth Peng.

•Same pattern in slaughter of sixty officers from Samrong: Interview with Sergeant Peou Tal.

•Reports of officers and civil servants executed at Japanese Agricultural Research Center: Interviews with Os Hoeung, Chhun Sun, Chheng Savan, farmer Dang Yim.

•Bloated bodies floating on Lake Boeum Thom: Interview with Norodom Vorapongs.

•Bodies of officers along railroad line near Svay Daunkeo: Interview with Nay Chea Sarunsarak.

•Bodies of 300 officers near village of Veal Trea: Interview with Sam Oeun.

•Putrefying bodies of hundreds of officers near village of O Koki: Interviews with Dang Yim and Os Hoeung.

•Site of another massacre at Bac Treng crossroads northwest of Battambang: Interview with Dang Yim.

•Communists boast of their killings and in some cases take people to see the dead: Interviews with accountant Lymeng Sanithvong, the monk Hem Samlaut, Sem Vann, Yen Savannary, teacher Chou Try's letter to Ponchaud.

•Return of eighty-eight pilots and their execution: Interviews with Lieutenant Sok Sambo, Ith Thaim, Chhun Sun; *Bangkok Post*, May 31, 1975; *Daily Telegraph* (London), June 25, 1975; *Chao Thai* (Bangkok), June 30, 1975; *Siam Rath* (Bangkok), July 2, 1975.

•Radio announcement that the returned pilots called "traitors" had been killed: Interview with Sok Sambo.

•Execution of blind beggar: Interview with Sar Sam.

•Conditions in the Soviet Hospital, Phnom Penh: Interview with Kem Phaly.

•Plan to eliminate prostitution and actual execution of some prostitutes: Interviews with Norodom Vorapongs and Chhun Sun. Statement of Tong Seng, a resident of Pailin, in *Testimonies on Genocide in Cambodia*, Bernard Hamel and Soth Polin (Item 4, July–August 1976, Paris).

•Execution of teachers at Wat Ek northwest of Battambang: Interview with Seng Lmouth; former Khmer Rouge soldier Tun Kar Nhet reported that intellectuals were all slated to die.

•Comrade Puth leads engineer Mon away to shoot him: Interview with Yen Savannary.

•Pogrom against intellectuals at first not executed as rigorously as against military personnel but widespread enough to make educated people hide fact of their education: Interviews with Ly Bun Heng, Seng Lmouth, Ea Than, Kyheng Savang, Norodom Vorapongs, Kem Phaly, Tun Kar Net; *Daily Telegraph* (London), April 18, 1976; *Le Monde* (Paris), February 17, 18, 1976.

•Arrest and slaughter of family of survivor of Mount Tippadei massacre: Interview with Phim Uon.

•Communists find and kill a government officer and his family: Interview with Kim Sath.

•Evacuation of Phum Kauk Lon and machine-gunning of its sixty families: Interview with Kim Sath.

•Sergeant Sreap Huot's escape from death is based on an interview with him at Kap Choeung in Surin Province, Thailand, on October 6, 1975.

•The report of about forty young women buried up to their necks east of Khal Kabei: interview with former soldier Doung Phal.

•The stabbing to death of sixty men, women and children at Mongkol Borei was reported by Ith Thaim in separate interviews with the authors.

CHAPTER IV

•The account of Tevi Rosa's journey and experiences is based on interviews with the child, her uncle, Ly Bun Heng, and Dr.

Vann Hay, who crossed the border into South Vietnam shortly before Ly and his group.

CHAPTER V

•Exposure of people of the exodus to extremes of weather: Interviews with Pisot Mao, Vann Hay, Kyheng Savang, Ho Mey, Thach Bun Rath and Kem Sos.

•Communist failure to organize water and food supplies or shelter for those on the journey: Interviews with Thiounn Kamel, Bo Penh, Ly Bun Heng, Pisot Mao, Ang Sokthan, Thach Bun Rath, Vong Khemerak, Siv Hav; New York Times editorial, July 9, 1975; AP report in Baltimore Sun, June 19, 1975.

•Two condensed milk cans equaling 500 grams or 1 pound: Interview with Mr. Senn, Asian distribution manager of Nestlé, in Vevey, Switzerland.

•Grim conditions even along rivers: Interview with Kyheng Savang, whose account is corroborated in interviews with Pisot Mao, Ang Sokthan, Yem Rithipol.

•The young and the old die first: Interviews with Kyheng Savang, Vann Hay, Pisot Mao, Ly Bun Heng.

•Comparable conditions during exodus from cities other than Phnom Penh: Interviews with Pin Sam Phon, Nhem Sary, Kuy Hong Taing, Ngy Duch, Lymeng Sanithvong, Peou Tal, Thiounn Kamel, Chorn Dayouth, Sar Sam, Sokh Kim Vang.

•Respite for the people during unguarded interludes: Interviews with Pa Sothy, Pisot Mao, Yem Rithipol, Thiounn Kamel, Ang Sokthan, Cham Kanya, Ly Bun Heng, Vann Hay.

•Contempt of communist soldiers for weak and thirsty: Interviews with university student Pa Sothy, Sem Vann, Pisot Mao.

•The prodding of laggards: Interviews with Vann Hay, Ho Mey, Ma Chheang, Sem Vann, Ea Than.

•Executions of laggards out of sight but within earshot of marchers: Interviews with Ea Than, Ho Mey.

•Execution for any sign of disobedience or protest: Interviews with Thiounn Kamel, Ho Mey, Ngy Duch, Tevi Rosa, Vann Hay, Dost Mohammed, Prach Chhea; Sunday Times (London), May 11, 1975.

•Experience of refugees at pagoda of Ta Phem and shooting of protester was reported by Prach Chhea.

•Machine-gunning of man in village of Rong Kor who asked

why they had to move: Interview with eyewitness Kuy Hong Taing.

•Unpredictable and pointless killing terrifies the people: Interviews with Ho Mey, Thiounn Kamel, Ngy Duch and gem prospector Ung Beng Chun.

•A communist soldier battered to death children of a government soldier's widow: Interview with seaman Chhung Khuor Min.

•Marchers throw away what they can no longer carry: Interviews with Ly Bun Heng, Pisot Mao.

•Communists establish marshaling centers further to relieve people of possessions: Interviews with Ho Mey, Kyheng Savang, Ith Thaim, Sam Poan, Ly Bun Heng, Yen Savannary.

•People try to keep automobiles even though they have to be pushed: Interviews with Pisot Mao, Yem Rithipol, Pech Kim Eng, Ly Bun Heng, Ang Sokthan, Tevi Rosa, Ho Mey.

•Communists commandeer cars at a radius of about 20 kilometers from capital: Interviews with Ku Soy Try, Siv Hav, Ung Sok Choeu, Kyheng Savang, Prach Chhea, who also reported killing of man protesting confiscation of automobile.

•Soldiers begin telling people they cannot go back but must work in rice paddies: Interviews with Yen Savannary, Bo Penh, Kyheng Savang, Ponchaud.

•Parted families search for each other: Interviews with Yem Rithipol, Ang Sokthan, Pisot Mao, Iem Ly Nuthy, Iem Tim Ravy.

•Suicide of middle-aged couple: Interview with Pisot Mao.

•Suicide of Chinese family of fifteen members: Interview with lawyer Ho Mey.

•Families unable to carry disabled or weak members decide to leave them behind: Interviews with Pisot Mao and Ang Sokthan. It was Ang who reported on how her group watched the airline stewardess and her husband decide to stay together.

•The effort to make farmers out of fishermen: Interview with Mrs. Mom Hol.

•The experience of Pailin residents who were driven north, then turned back and then driven north again: Interviews with Chorn Dayouth and Ung Beng Chun.

•Angka Loeu commissars begin telling people to return to their native villages: Interviews with Yen Savannary, Thiounn Kamel, Peou Tal.

•Refugees having surrendered identity papers were able to

claim village of their choice as native village: Interviews with Ly Bun Heng, Vann Hay, Cham Kanya.

•Sooner or later, however, a communist commissar would haul people off roads and send them to new settlement: Interviews with Ngy Duch, Vann Hay, Ly Bun Heng, Yen Savannary.

CHAPTER VI

•The account of Ngy Duch's experiences after being driven from Pailin to the new village of Ampil Pram Daum is based on extensive interviews with him in Thailand and later in France.

•Description of the New Villages and their work patterns: Interviews with Ngy Duch, salesman Peou Yama, student Peou Sophal, farmer Peou Sophleah, Kuy Hong Taing, Norodom Vorapongs, Vann Hay, Ea Than, Sem Vann, Yen Savannary, Ung Beng Chun, Ang Sokthan, barber Kim Houl, Bo Penh, Sergeant Ouk Phon, Dap Youn, farmer Nhek Khem, photographer Keat Vannak, farmer Yib Meng, Chou Try, Kyheng Savang, Pin Sam Phon, Chheng Savan, Phal Oudam, Chorn Dayouth, Sam Oeun, Os Hoeung, Ly Bun Heng, Kem Phaly, Sokh Kim Vang, Phal So Vichet, Young Phorn, gemstone cutter Yan Nam; New York Times, January 21, 1976.

•Ideological lectures in the evening and the ceremony known as kosang: Interviews with Ngy Duch, Ly Bun Heng, Yen Savannary, Phal So Vichet, Young Phorn, Ung Beng Chun, farmer Karn Sdoeurng, Sam Oeun, Chorn Dayouth.

•Revolutionary education and the slogans learned by rote: Interviews with Ly Bun Heng, Ngy Duch, Ang Sokthan, Ouk Phon, Sem Vann, Tevi Rosa, Vann Hay, Phal Oudam, Bo Penh, Thach Bun Rath, Yen Savannary, Ku Soy Try and Nhek Khem.

•References to the Wheel of History (Kang Prawattisastr): Interviews with Ngy Duch and Ang Sokthan.

•The threat to send someone to Angka Loeu for reeducation: Interviews with Ouk Phon and Tevi Rosa.

•Severe strictures against sex: Interviews with Phal Oudam, Yen Savannary, Phal So Vichet, former CARE employee Meas Rattana, Ung Beng Chun, Pa Sothy and Vann Hay, who reported the communist commissar's statement at a special meeting called to discuss sex.

•Effort to break up traditional family relationships and brainwashing of children: Interviews with Phal So Vichet, Vann Hay, Ngy Duch, Pa Sothy, Chorn Dayouth, Ung Sok Choeu, Prach Chhea; *Sunday Times* (London), April 18, 1976.

•Separation or execution of couples caught arguing more than twice: Interviews with Ngy Duch and Vann Hay.

•Rice ration after evacuation of cities and gradual decrease of ration: Interviews with Kyheng Savang, Chorn Dayouth, Hem Samlaut, Ngy Duch; Chou Try letter; *Guardian* (Manchester), February 9, 11, 13, April 6, 13, 15, 1976; *Sunday Telegraph* (London), August 15, 1976.

•Villagers augment diet with anything edible: Interviews with Young Phorn, Pin Sam Phon, Sem Vann, Ngy Duch, Ea Than, Keo Su Wan and Ung Beng Chun; Chou Try letter.

•Food shortage reached famine proportions by late August: Interviews with Keo Kim Taun, Yen Savannary, Pech Kim Eng, Yan Nam; Chou Try letter; *Daily Telegraph* (London), April 8, 1976; *Time*, Asia Edition, April 26, 1976; *Guardian* (Manchester), February 9, 11, 13 and April 6, 13, 15, 1976.

•The situation in the New Village of Beng Katom was reported in detail by Yan Nam.

•No effort made to save orphaned children of little use to *Angka*: Chou Try letter; interviews with Yen Savannary, Ith Thaim.

•High death rate owing to disease, malnutrition, lack of medical care or hygiene: Interviews with Ngy Duch, Phal So Vichet, Kem Phaly, Phal Oudam, Pech Kim Eng, mechanic Ong Por Yeng, Keat Vannak, Kim Houl, soldier Roeung Phuon, Keo Kim Taun, Chou Try letter; *Los Angeles Times*, August 12, 1975; *Sunday Telegraph* (London), August 15, 1976; *Time*, Asia Edition, April 26, 1976.

•The situation in Soeur, an established village, was reported by Keo Kim Taun. Farmer Pherm Houn also reported on life in an established village.

•*Angka Loeu* finally established makeshift dispensaries: Letter from Chou Try; interview with Keo Su Wan.

•*Angka's* two forms of punishment are *kosang* and execution: Interviews with Sokh Kim Vang, Ngy Duch, Norodom Vorapongs, Young Phorn, Kuy Hong Taing, Yen Savannary, Hem Samlaut, Ouk Phon, Phal So Vichet.

•Execution of those who try to escape or who disobey orders: Interviews with Phal So Vichet, Roeung Phuon, Pherm Houn, Sem Vann, Ea Than.

•No warnings to former Lon Nol military personnel or gendarmerie: Interviews with Chorn Dayouth, Os Hoeung, Pherm Houn, Keat Vannak, Sem Vann, Phal Oudam, Karn Sdoeurng, Chheng Savan.

•Executions increasingly conducted in public and bodies are exhibited: Interviews with Hem Samlaut, Ngy Duch, Sar Sam, Kim Houl, student Yep Chay, Bo Penh, Pa Sothy, Lymeng Sanithvong, Chheng Savan.

CHAPTER VII

•The second migration: Interviews with Ang Sokthan, welfare worker Hok Saaem; New York *Times*, January 21, 1976; *Le Monde* (Paris), February 17, 1976.

•Refugees not allowed to enjoy the harvest: Interviews with Ouk Phon, Nhek Khem, Keat Vannak, Yan Nam, Ang Sokthan.

•The account of Ang Sokthan's experiences is based on lengthy interviews with her.

CHAPTER VIII

•Sem Vann's escape was described by him in an interview in France at which Father Rondineau was present. Father Rondineau described Sem as decent, gentle and intelligent. At that time Sem gave a demonstration of how to use nail clippers as a tool.

•*Angka Loeu* executes those who try to escape: Interviews with farmer Chen Yed, Phal So Vichet, Hem Samlaut, Lymeng Sanithvong, Chheng Savan, trader Sok Yom, soldier Morn Sophon.

•Mines and booby traps seal off the borders: Interviews with Phal Oudam, Young Phorn, Chheng Savan.

•Patrols ambush and kill escapees in border area: Interview with Keo Kim Taun; *Siam Rath* (Bangkok), July 2, 1975; Bangkok *Post*, July 14, 1975; Washington *Post*, August 21, 1975; New York *Times*, July 21, 1975; Washington *Post*, July 21, 1975 and January 17, 1976.

•Fathers strangle their babies so communists cannot hear their cries: Interview with Os Hoeung, who was with the fathers. Ung Beng Chun reported a similar case.

•Communists kill other small children who could not walk fast enough: Interview with Os Hoeung.

•The escape of Chen Yed and the 1,806 villagers is based on an interview with Chen; the basic outline of his account was confirmed by Thai authorities whom the authors interviewed.

•The escape of the four young men in a stolen Mercedes is based on interviews with two of them in Thailand and later in France.

•Major Phim gave details of his escape from the Tippadei massacre and then from Cambodia into Thailand in an interview with Anthony Paul. Later Ponchaud interviewed a friend of the major's and learned Major Phim had returned to Cambodia and been killed.

•Nhek Khem's escape is based on an interview in Thailand.

•The sights and smells of the jungles: Interviews with Corporal Mohammed Hamid, Ouk Phon, Chorn Dayouth.

•The safe end to Ngy Duch's journey is based on his own account given in Thailand and France.

CHAPTER IX

•Second migration completed and New Villages functioning: Washington *Star*, January 21, 1976; Sunday *Times* (London), April 18, 1976.

•Foreigners including longtime residents of Vietnamese descent expelled: Interview with Kenneth Quinn, National Security Council.

•Radio monitors intercept orders to exterminate all former officials: This information was obtained confidentially from three different foreign intelligence agencies.

•Communist plans to round up all former civil servants, teachers, soldiers, village chiefs, ward chiefs and students: Interviews with teacher Non Chy Moc Ra, soldier Sou Sam You L, soldier Thi Champarith; Chou Try letter; *Time*, Asia Edition, April 26, 1976; *Le Monde* (Paris), February 17, 18, 1976.

•The report about engineer You was given by teacher Long Samouth.

•Thai Ministry of the Interior statement regarding new purges: interviews by authors with Thai authorities, Bangkok.

•The odyssey of Dr. Oum Nal: Interviews with the doctor in France.

•Quote about banishing everything of the old society: Interview with Meas Rattana.

•Glorification of teenage girl named Phali: Interview with former teacher Sam Yang.

•The first harvest "not a bumper crop, but sufficient for self-supply," comes from the interview former Premier Pol Pot granted the deputy editor of the Vietnam News Agency on July 20, 1976; FBIS, July 27, 1976.

•Pockets of hunger persist: Interviews with teacher Song Chin Eth, Major Dura Narin, who also reported on the dreaded new malady of "memory sickness."

•Punishment more swift for presumed malingering: Interview with former newsman Sou Satray.

•*Angka Loeu* harshened restrictions on courtship and marriage: Interviews with Dura Narin, Sou Satray, student Klod Viet; *Sunday Times* (London), January 25, 1976.

•Lewis Simons' report was published in the Washington *Post*, November 12, 1976.

•Estimates of number who died after peace came to Cambodia: Interviews with Ponchaud and Jon Swain; Yves-Guy Berges report for *France Soir*, which was distributed by the Associated Press and published in the New York *Times*, June 3, 1976; *Famiglia Cristiana*, September 26, 1976 (Paola Brianti's interview with Khieu Samphan); *Sunday Times* (London), May 11, 1975; interviews with Oum Nal, Siv Sichan, Carney, Quinn, *Area Handbook* (which gave strength of Cambodian republican forces); Anthony Paul's interviews with Thai officials and foreign diplomats in Bangkok; telephone interview with James McHale of the Voice of America; *Le Monde* (Paris), February 17, 18, 1976, printed in *Congressional Record—Senate*, April 7, 1976.

•Pol Pot's interview with Tran Thanh Xuan, deputy editor in chief of the Vietnam News Agency, was broadcast (in English) from Ho Chi Minh City (Saigon) to the Vietnam News Agency office in Hanoi at 0730 GMT July 27, 1976, and made public by FBIS.

•Ieng Sary goes to United Nations: FBIS, Peking, North China News Agency, in English, August 31, 1975; James Baker, Economic Affairs Division, United States Mission to United Nations.

•*Angka Loeu* speaks to the people from Radio Phnom Penh: Ponchaud in *Le Monde* (Paris), February 17, 18, 1976, reported what those broadcasts said beginning early 1976. English translation of Ponchaud article appears on page S5086 of *Congressional Record*, April 7, 1976.

•*Angka Loeu*'s song on Radio Phnom Penh, autumn 1976: *South China Morning Post* (Hong Kong) November 7, 1976; New York *Times*, November 14, 1976.

•World remains silent about events in Cambodia: Speech of James Russell Wiggins, former editor of the Washington *Post*, in Worcester, Massachusetts, following Sigma Delta Chi ceremonies, which was reprinted in *Editor and Publisher*, August 23, 1975; remarks of Leo Cherne, chairman of executive committee of Freedom House, printed in *Congressional Record*, September 17, 1975; former Prime Minister In Tam's appeal to the Secretary General of the United Nations, September 22, 1975; editorial, New York *Times*, October 20, 1975; Allan C. Brownfeld's "West's Double Standards" in Lima *News*, August 24, 1976, and printed in *Congressional Record*, September 14, 1976; John P. Roche, "Unmourned and Unreported," *Free Trade Union News*, Vol. 31, No. 9, September 1976; New Orleans *Times-Picayune*, April 21, 1976 (Patrick J. Buchanan).

ADDITIONAL READINGS

Burchett, Wilfred. *Second Indochina War*. New York: International Publishers, 1970.

Chandler, David P. "Changing Cambodia." *Current History* (December 1970).

Communism in Indochina, Joseph J. Zasloff and MacAlister Brown, eds. Lexington Books. New York: D. C. Heath Co., 1975.

Hall, D. G. E. *A History of Southeast Asia*, 3rd ed. New York: Macmillan, 1968.

Kirk, Donald. *Wider War: The Struggle for Cambodia, Thailand and Laos*. New York: Praeger, 1971.

Lehman, John. *The Executive, Congress and Foreign Policy*. New York: Praeger, 1976.

Marschall, Walther F. Baron von. *Seabury House Papers Royal Defense College Studies*. London: 1975.

Meyer, Charles, *Derrière le Sourire Khmer*. Paris: Plon, 1971.

Osborne, Milton. *Politics and Power in Cambodia*. New York: Longman, 1974.

Sihanouk, Norodom, as related to Wilfred Burchett. *My War with the CIA*. New York: Pantheon Books, 1973.

Simon, Sheldon W. *War and Politics in Cambodia*. Durham, N.C.: Duke University Press, 1974.

Steinberg, David J., et al. *In Search of Southeast Asia*. New York: Praeger, 1971.

also

Department of State. *The Cambodia Strike: Defensive Action for Peace*. Pub. 8529. [President's Report to the Nation of April 30.] Washington, D.C.: U.S. Government Printing Office, 1970.

Department of State. *Cambodia in Perspective: Vietnamization Assured*. Pub. 8536. [President's Interim Report to the Nation of June 3.] Washington, D.C.: U.S. Government Printing Office, 1970.

INDEX

As noted in the Preface, p. xv, the surname precedes the given name in the Khmer language, so that in this index the name Ung Sok Choeu, for example, is not inverted as in Western usage but appears under the letter U as Ung Sok Choeu, not under the letter C as Choeu, Ung Sok.